INTRODUCTION: MERGING PATHS OF BLOCKCHAIN AND PURPOSE-DRIVEN ESG LEADERSHIP

CHAPTER 1: UNDERSTANDING BLOCKCHAIN'S ROLE IN ESG FRAMEWORKS

CHAPTER 2: BLOCKCHAIN AS A TOOL FOR TRANSFORMATIVE SOCIAL INNOVATION

CHAPTER 3: LEVERAGING BLOCKCHAIN FOR ENVIRONMENTAL SUSTAINABILITY

CHAPTER 4: ADVANCING SOCIAL EQUITY WITH BLOCKCHAIN TECHNOLOGY

CHAPTER 5: GOVERNANCE ISSUES, ETHICAL LEADERSHIP CHALLENGES IN CRYPTOCURRENCY

CHAPTER 6: VISION AND PURPOSE: GUIDING BLOCKCHAIN ADOPTION

CHAPTER 7: BUILDING RESILIENCE IN THE FACE OF BLOCKCHAIN CHALLENGES

CHAPTER 8: LEADING THROUGH CHANGE AND FOSTERING ADAPTABILITY WITHIN THE BLOCKCHAIN ECOSYSTEM

CHAPTER 9: COMMUNICATING THE IMPACT: BLOCKCHAIN AND ESG NARRATIVES

CHAPTER 10: THE FUTURE OF PURPOSE-DRIVEN BLOCKCHAIN LEADERSHIP

Introduction: Merging Paths of Blockchain and Purpose-Driven ESG Leadership

In today's rapidly evolving digital landscape, blockchain technology emerges not just as a groundbreaking innovation in finance and data management but as a powerful ally in advancing Environmental, Social, and Governance (ESG) leadership. At its core, blockchain is a decentralized ledger technology that facilitates secure, transparent, and tamper-proof transactions. This intrinsic nature of blockchain offers a unique intersection with ESG principles, promising transformative solutions to some of the most pressing global challenges.

Environmental stewardship is a critical component of today's business landscape, and blockchain technology offers significant advancements in how companies can manage their environmental impact through enhanced transparency and efficiency. One of the most transformative applications of blockchain lies in supply chain management. By integrating blockchain technology, companies are able to establish a fully transparent supply chain that traces the environmental footprint of products from their origin to the end consumer. This level of transparency empowers consumers to make more informed purchasing decisions and encourages companies to adopt and maintain sustainable practices by holding them accountable to their environmental claims.

Blockchain technology enables companies to optimize the use of resources and reduce waste through more effective asset management systems. By providing a reliable and immutable record of asset use and disposal, blockchain helps organizations identify inefficiencies and areas for improvement in their resource management processes. This can lead to significant reductions in waste and energy consumption, contributing directly to a decrease in the organization's overall environmental impact.

The application of blockchain in environmental stewardship extends beyond supply chain management. It can also support the implementation of more sophisticated systems for monitoring environmental data and ensuring compliance with regulatory requirements. For instance, blockchain can be used to track emissions data accurately or to manage trading systems for carbon credits. This technology ensures that all recorded data is accurate and tamper-proof, enhancing the accountability of reporting and compliance processes.

The integration of blockchain technology into environmental management practices allows companies not only to enhance operational efficiencies but also to build trust with consumers and regulators. As businesses face increasing pressure to demonstrate their commitment to sustainable practices, blockchain stands out as a tool that can help bridge the gap between environmental goals and business operations, leading to more sustainable, transparent, and efficient practices.

Blockchain technology holds transformative potential for fostering social equity by addressing and mitigating disparities and inequities both within and across societies. This technology offers a robust platform for financial inclusion, particularly through decentralized finance (DeFi) solutions. DeFi systems operate independently of traditional financial infrastructures, such as banks, which often exclude significant portions of the population due to geographical barriers or lack of formal identification. By providing essential financial services directly through blockchain platforms, individuals who are unbanked or underbanked can gain access to tools for savings, loans, insurance, and other critical financial services without the need for intermediaries. This accessibility is crucial for economic empowerment and offers a pathway out of poverty for millions worldwide.

In addition to financial inclusion, blockchain technology is pioneering solutions in digital identity. Blockchain-based identity systems offer a secure, immutable, and user-controlled method of storing personal data. These systems allow individuals to maintain control over their personal information and decide how and with whom their data is shared. For populations such as refugees or those without government-issued IDs, having a verifiable digital identity can provide access to services like healthcare, voting, and legal systems, which are often out of reach without traditional forms of ID.

Blockchain's impact on social equity extends into sectors like healthcare and education, where it supports broader inclusivity and access. In healthcare, blockchain can securely store patient records, ensuring they are easily accessible by authorized healthcare providers regardless of the patient's location or economic status. This system not only streamlines medical care but also protects patient privacy and improves the accuracy of medical records across borders and healthcare systems.

In the field of education, blockchain can be utilized to verify qualifications and academic records, reducing fraud and making it easier for qualifications to be recognized internationally. This has significant implications for students from lower-income countries or conflict zones, enabling them to prove their educational background and pursue further education or employment opportunities globally.

Blockchain also facilitates community engagement initiatives by providing transparent platforms for voting and public consultations. These platforms can ensure that every voice is heard and counted in a secure and transparent manner, promoting greater participation in community decision-making and governance.

Blockchain's role in promoting social equity is multifaceted and powerful. By providing tools for financial inclusion, secure identity management, and greater access to essential services, blockchain technology is creating opportunities for a more inclusive society where disparities are addressed head-on, and individuals are empowered to improve their socioeconomic conditions. This aligns with broader global efforts to achieve social equity and inclusivity, marking blockchain as a key player in the movement towards a fairer world.

On the governance front, blockchain technology's inherent capabilities are profoundly aligned with the principles of integrity, transparency, and accountability—core elements of the "Governance" aspect in ESG (Environmental, Social, and Governance) frameworks. These features of blockchain provide transformative potential for enhancing how entities, from corporations to governments, manage and report their activities, thereby building trust and facilitating ethical governance practices.

At its core, blockchain technology offers a decentralized ledger that records transactions in an immutable manner. This means once data is entered into the blockchain, it cannot be altered or deleted, ensuring the integrity of the data throughout its lifecycle. This characteristic is especially crucial in environments where data authenticity is paramount, such as financial transactions, legal agreements, and corporate records. By maintaining an unalterable record of all transactions, blockchain technology significantly reduces the opportunities for fraud and data tampering.

Blockchain facilitates the automation of transactions through smart contracts, which are self-executing contracts with the terms of the agreement directly written into lines of code. These contracts automatically enforce and execute the terms of agreements based on predefined rules and triggers, without human intervention, thereby minimizing the risk of mismanagement or manipulation. This automation not only streamlines processes but also embeds a high level of accountability and precision in operations such as fund disbursements, compliance reporting, and benefit allocations.

In corporate governance, blockchain can radically enhance how decisions are made and recorded. For instance, blockchain can be used to streamline the voting processes during shareholder meetings. By using blockchain-based voting systems, companies can ensure that each vote is securely cast and immutably recorded, making the results transparent and immediately verifiable. This system not only enhances shareholder engagement by making participation easier and more secure but also strengthens the integrity of the voting process itself.

Blockchain enables real-time reporting and auditing of corporate actions, which can be especially useful for complex regulatory compliance that requires rigorous and ongoing disclosure. With blockchain, companies can provide regulators and stakeholders with a live, transparent view of their operational adherence to required standards, thereby improving compliance monitoring and enforcement. The transparency and accountability offered by blockchain are vital for building and maintaining trust among stakeholders. In an era where corporate transparency is a significant concern, and public trust is hard to earn, blockchain provides a verifiable and secure method to disclose operations and internal processes. For stakeholders, from investors to customers and regulators, accessing blockchain-based disclosures and records provides a higher degree of confidence in the veracity of the information provided and the ethical standards of the company.

Thus, blockchain's role in governance is multifaceted and immensely impactful. By ensuring data integrity, automating transactions to enforce accountability, and enhancing transparency in corporate governance, blockchain technology can help mitigate risks associated with fraud, corruption, and mismanagement. This technological approach not only supports more robust governance models but also aligns with global efforts to foster business environments that prioritize ethics and transparency, crucial for sustainable and equitable growth.

The intersection of blockchain technology with ESG leadership is not merely theoretical. Numerous initiatives and projects across the globe are harnessing blockchain to drive sustainable success. For example, renewable energy trading platforms use blockchain to enable the peer-to-peer sale of surplus renewable energy, incentivizing the production and consumption of green energy. Similarly, blockchain is being utilized to create more transparent and efficient carbon credit markets, directly contributing to environmental sustainability efforts.

Blockchain technology's compatibility with ESG principles represents a frontier of opportunity for leaders committed to sustainability, social responsibility, and ethical governance. As we delve deeper into the potential applications of blockchain across ESG domains, it becomes increasingly clear that this technology offers a set of tools not just for business innovation but for social and environmental transformation. The challenge and opportunity for today's leaders lie in harnessing this potential responsibly, ensuring that blockchain serves as a catalyst for positive change in alignment with the broader goals of ESG leadership.

The rapid evolution of blockchain and cryptocurrency technologies presents a unique set of challenges and opportunities that necessitate a new kind of leadership: purpose-driven leadership. This form of leadership is not only visionary and innovative but also deeply rooted in ethical principles, sustainability, and social responsibility. As these technologies continue to disrupt traditional business models and societal norms, the need for leaders who can navigate these changes with a strong moral compass and a commitment to the greater good becomes increasingly imperative.

Navigating the ethical and regulatory landscapes of blockchain and cryptocurrency presents a significant challenge due to the rapidly evolving nature of these technologies and their applications. The environment is characterized by a patchwork of regulatory standards across different jurisdictions and a series of complex ethical dilemmas that arise from the decentralized nature of these technologies. In this context, the role of purpose-driven leadership becomes crucial as these leaders steer their projects through these turbulent waters, ensuring that technological innovation aligns with ethical standards and social values.

Blockchain and cryptocurrency projects often disrupt established norms and systems, raising a spectrum of ethical issues. For instance, the anonymity provided by blockchain can protect privacy and security but also raises concerns about accountability and the potential for misuse, such as money laundering or financing illegal activities. Purpose-driven leaders must engage in continuous ethical evaluation, examining how the technologies impact stakeholders and considering long-term societal implications. They must ensure that the benefits of these technologies, such as increased accessibility to financial services, do not come at the cost of ethical transgressions or exacerbating existing inequalities.

One of the most critical roles for leaders within the blockchain and cryptocurrency sectors is advocacy for effective regulation that accommodates the unique aspects of these technologies. Regulatory frameworks can lag behind technological advances, leading to gaps that may be exploited unethically. Leaders must work closely with regulators to develop laws and guidelines that protect consumers and ensure fair practices while still allowing room for innovation and growth. This involves clarifying the application of existing laws to new technologies, as well as advocating for new regulations that address emerging issues directly related to blockchain and cryptocurrency.

Purpose-driven leaders champion transparency as a fundamental principle in their operations to build trust among users, investors, and regulators. Implementing systems that track and verify transactions on a blockchain can help demystify the technology for regulators and the public, promoting broader acceptance and integration into mainstream finance. Additionally, leaders must ensure that consumer protection is at the forefront of blockchain and cryptocurrency initiatives, implementing measures to protect users from fraud, theft, and other risks associated with digital transactions.

In an industry prone to rapid changes and innovation, maintaining healthy competition is essential. Leaders need to advocate for and adhere to practices that prevent monopolistic structures and promote a diverse ecosystem of blockchain applications and services. This not only aids in fostering innovation but also ensures that no single entity can wield too much power or influence, which could stifle technological progress and fair market practices.

Given the global nature of blockchain and cryptocurrencies, leaders must also navigate the international regulatory landscape. This includes understanding and complying with international sanctions, anti-money laundering (AML) standards, and cross-border data privacy regulations. Engaging in international forums and collaborative regulatory discussions can help harmonize standards and practices across borders, facilitating smoother operations and broader adoption of blockchain technology.

Purpose-driven leaders within the blockchain and cryptocurrency fields are vital in navigating the complex ethical and regulatory landscapes. By advocating for thoughtful regulations, promoting transparency, protecting consumers, ensuring healthy competition, and engaging in international cooperation, these leaders can help harness the positive potential of blockchain and cryptocurrencies while mitigating risks and ensuring that innovation does not compromise ethical standards or societal values.

Despite the significant potential of blockchain and cryptocurrency, these technologies face substantial trust barriers among the general public and traditional financial institutions. Purpose-driven leadership plays a crucial role in overcoming these hurdles by actively demonstrating the positive social and environmental impacts that these technologies can achieve. Leaders in this space can effectively change perceptions and foster broader adoption by strategically prioritizing projects that deliver tangible societal and environmental benefits.

For instance, by focusing on blockchain projects that enhance financial inclusion, leaders can illustrate how these technologies provide essential financial services to underserved populations. This not only helps in reducing inequality but also supports economic development in regions where traditional banking infrastructure is lacking or non-existent. Similarly, by leveraging blockchain to track and reduce carbon emissions, leaders can address urgent environmental issues such as climate change. This not only shows blockchain's utility beyond financial applications but also aligns it with global efforts towards sustainability.

Integrating blockchain into the supply chain can ensure fair trade practices by providing transparent tracking of products from origin to consumer. This level of transparency allows consumers to make informed choices about the products they buy, ensuring that their purchases support ethical practices. Such applications of blockchain technology reinforce its potential to create significant positive impacts in various sectors, thereby fostering trust among skeptical stakeholders and encouraging wider adoption.

Purpose-driven leaders are essential in showcasing how blockchain and cryptocurrency can address some of the world's most pressing challenges, from financial disparity to environmental degradation. By focusing on projects with clear benefits and openly communicating these impacts, leaders can transform public and institutional perceptions, paving the way for increased trust and widespread adoption of these transformative technologies.

The decentralized nature of blockchain and the anonymity provided by cryptocurrencies introduce a range of ethical considerations that must be carefully managed. Purpose-driven leaders in the blockchain and cryptocurrency sectors are crucial for ensuring that these powerful technologies are used responsibly and ethically. Their role involves more than just overseeing technological development; they must also guide the ethical deployment of these technologies to ensure they benefit society as a whole.

To achieve this, leaders must develop and implement robust frameworks and standards that prevent the misuse of blockchain and cryptocurrencies. For instance, without proper oversight, these technologies could be used for money laundering or financing illicit activities. To combat such risks, leaders need to establish clear guidelines that are rigorously enforced to prevent misuse. This includes mechanisms for tracking transactions in a way that balances the need for privacy with the necessity of preventing illegal activities.

Protecting user privacy and data security is paramount in fostering trust and wider adoption of blockchain technologies. Leaders must ensure that systems are in place to protect sensitive information from breaches, which involves implementing advanced security measures and constantly updating them to address new vulnerabilities. By setting high ethical standards and fostering a culture of integrity, leaders can guide the development of blockchain and cryptocurrency in a direction that aligns with broader societal values. This includes promoting transparency where it is needed, ensuring fairness in how services are delivered, and maintaining accountability by those who operate and govern these technological systems.

In guiding ethical innovation, it is also important for leaders to engage with a range of stakeholders, including regulators, consumers, and the wider community, to ensure that diverse perspectives are considered in the development of blockchain technologies. This collaborative approach helps ensure that the evolution of blockchain and cryptocurrencies reflects a consensus on ethical standards, rather than the interests of a select few.

Guiding ethical innovation in blockchain and cryptocurrency is a complex but crucial responsibility that requires purpose-driven leadership committed to upholding and advancing societal values. Through thoughtful oversight, collaborative engagement, and a commitment to ethical practices, leaders can steer these transformative technologies toward outcomes that are not only innovative and efficient but also equitable and beneficial for all.

Blockchain and cryptocurrency technologies have faced significant scrutiny over their environmental impacts, especially concerning the high energy consumption required by some blockchain networks like Bitcoin. This has sparked a growing need for purpose-driven leadership that actively champions sustainability within the blockchain space. Such leadership is not only about driving technological advancements but also about ensuring that these technologies are developed and used in environmentally responsible ways.

Purpose-driven leaders are pivotal in promoting the adoption of more energy-efficient consensus mechanisms such as proof-of-stake, which requires significantly less energy compared to the traditional proof-of-work systems used in many current cryptocurrencies. By advocating for and implementing these greener alternatives, leaders can significantly reduce the carbon footprint of their blockchain operations.

Beyond just improving energy efficiency, these leaders can also harness blockchain technology to support broader environmental conservation efforts. For example, blockchain can enhance the transparency and accountability of environmental projects through better tracking of carbon credits and more effective monitoring of renewable energy usage. This can help ensure that environmental initiatives are not only proposed but actively pursued and accurately reported, enhancing the overall impact of these efforts.

Leaders in this field have the unique opportunity to redefine what success looks like in the industry. Instead of focusing solely on profitability or market dominance, they can shift the narrative towards sustainability and the contribution of blockchain technology to a sustainable future. This involves setting new benchmarks for success that include ecological impact assessments and sustainability goals. By taking a proactive stance on these issues, leaders can help mitigate the negative perceptions of blockchain's environmental impact and position their organizations at the forefront of a movement towards sustainable digital innovation. This not only benefits the planet but also adds a valuable dimension to their brand's identity and appeal, particularly among increasingly environmentally conscious consumers and investors.

In championing sustainability, purpose-driven leaders not only pave the way for more responsible use of blockchain technology but also inspire others in the industry to follow suit. This collective effort is essential for ensuring that the revolutionary potential of blockchain and cryptocurrency is realized in a way that contributes positively to our planet's health and future sustainability.

At the core of purpose-driven leadership within the blockchain and cryptocurrency sectors is a profound commitment to leveraging innovation for social good. Leaders with this focus recognize that while technological advancements can drive significant disruption, they must also be harnessed to address real-world challenges, improve lives, and foster a more equitable and sustainable global community. This approach goes beyond merely capitalizing on technological trends; it involves shaping these innovations in ways that contribute positively to society.

Purpose-driven leaders view technology not just as a tool for economic gain but as a means to solve pressing societal issues. Whether it's enhancing financial inclusion through decentralized financial services that reach underserved populations, or using blockchain for transparent supply chains that promote fairness and reduce environmental impact, these leaders seek to apply technology in ways that provide tangible benefits to all, not just a select few.

The need for such leadership is particularly pressing in the fast-evolving realms of blockchain and cryptocurrency. These fields are not only rapidly advancing but are also uniquely positioned to influence wide sectors of society and business due to their foundational capabilities in security, transparency, and efficiency. As blockchain technologies continue to develop and become more integrated into mainstream business operations and societal functions, the role of visionary leaders becomes all the more critical.

These leaders are tasked with steering the blockchain and cryptocurrency innovations toward outcomes that uphold and promote social values. Their ability to anticipate the implications of new technologies and guide their application reflects their commitment to ethical practices and their understanding of the broader impact of their decisions.

The leaders who excel in this environment will be those who combine a clear vision with a steadfast ethical compass. Their strategies and actions will need to align with principles that prioritize the well-being of society and the planet. This might mean advocating for and implementing energy-efficient blockchain solutions to counteract the environmental concerns associated with some cryptocurrency operations, or it could involve developing platforms that enhance access to essential services for marginalized communities.

As blockchain and cryptocurrency technologies continue to mature and reshape industries, the leaders at the helm of these innovations will play a pivotal role in defining their trajectory. Their commitment to integrating ethical considerations with business and technological strategies will be crucial in harnessing the full potential of these digital advancements. Ultimately, the legacy of blockchain and cryptocurrency will depend significantly on these leaders' ability to bridge the gap between cutting-edge technology and the enduring pursuit of global social good, ensuring that the digital revolution benefits humanity as a whole.

Chapter 1: Understanding Blockchain's Role in ESG Frameworks

Blockchain technology, at its core, is a decentralized digital ledger that records transactions across multiple computers in such a manner that the registered transactions cannot be altered retroactively. This technology underpins cryptocurrencies like Bitcoin, but its potential extends far beyond just digital currencies. By offering a secure and transparent way to record transactions, blockchain technology presents a radical departure from traditional centralized record-keeping systems.

Decentralization and transparency are cornerstones of blockchain technology, offering a radical shift from traditional centralized systems. In blockchain systems, the ledger is distributed across an entire network of computers, known as nodes, rather than being controlled by a single central authority. This distribution means that each participant, or node, in the network maintains a copy of the entire database, including its full transaction history. As a result, the data on a blockchain is not stored in any single location or controlled by any single entity, which democratizes access and control over the information.

This decentralized nature of blockchain fundamentally changes how data is handled and verified. Since every node in the network has access to the entire chain, they can see and verify all the transactions independently. This transparency is critical as it allows for open verification of the data by any participant in the network, enhancing the trustworthiness and security of the data. Moreover, when a new transaction is made, it must be approved by the network through a consensus process before it is added to the blockchain. This process ensures that each transaction is agreed upon by multiple nodes, preventing any single entity from exerting control over the transaction data.

The transparency provided by blockchain does more than just facilitate trust among network participants; it also builds a system that is inherently resistant to fraud and corruption. In a traditional centralized system, data can be altered or deleted without the knowledge of other participants. In contrast, the blockchain ledger is immutable, meaning that once a transaction is recorded, it cannot be changed or removed. This immutability is safeguarded by the consensus mechanism, which requires agreement from multiple nodes to alter any information on the blockchain. Any attempt to alter transaction data by a single party would be immediately evident to other users, who can see such attempts and reject them.

Blockchain's transparency extends beyond mere transaction data. It can encompass the execution of contracts, the transfer of assets, and compliance with regulations. This makes it an ideal technology for applications where transparency and integrity of data are crucial, such as in financial services, supply chain management, and regulatory compliance. In these fields, blockchain can not only reduce the risk of fraud but also streamline operations by providing a clear, auditable trail of all transactions and interactions.

The decentralization and transparency inherent in blockchain technology foster a more open, trustworthy, and secure environment for conducting transactions. This environment encourages a reduction in fraud, enhances security, and builds a foundation of trust that traditional centralized systems struggle to match. As blockchain technology continues to evolve, its potential to transform various sectors through its fundamental principles of decentralization and transparency becomes increasingly evident, promising a future where data integrity and openness are paramount.

Immutability is a fundamental aspect of blockchain technology that underpins its security and reliability. This characteristic means that once data or a transaction has been recorded on the blockchain, it cannot be altered or deleted, effectively making the blockchain a permanent, unchangeable record of transactions. This permanence is critical for applications where the integrity of data is paramount, such as in financial transactions, legal documents, and other sensitive information.

The immutability of blockchain is achieved through the use of cryptographic hashes, which are algorithms that convert data into a fixed-size string of characters, which is virtually impossible to reverse-engineer. Each block in a blockchain contains a unique cryptographic hash of the previous block, along with its own transaction data and time stamp. This creates a chronological chain of blocks, or a blockchain. If an attempt is made to alter the transaction data within a block, the cryptographic hash for that block would change. Since each block is linked to the hash of the previous block, altering one block would necessitate alterations to all subsequent blocks in the chain, which is computationally impractical to achieve, especially on large, well-distributed blockchains.

This unbreakable chain of hashes ensures that once a block is added to the blockchain, it becomes immutable. This immutability guarantees the integrity of the data stored on the blockchain, as any change to the data would be immediately obvious to all participants in the network. It also means that all transactions are transparent and verifiable by any user at any time, adding a layer of security and trust that is not possible with traditional, mutable record-keeping systems.

Immutability also plays a crucial role in non-financial applications. For instance, in supply chain management, blockchain can be used to create an immutable record of the origin, journey, and handling of products. This can help in verifying the authenticity of products, ensuring compliance with regulatory requirements, and preventing fraud. Similarly, in the realm of intellectual property, artists and creators can use blockchain to register their works, creating an immutable proof of ownership and timestamp that can help in protecting their rights.

The immutability of blockchain is invaluable in regulatory compliance and auditing processes. Because changes to data are both traceable and permanent, auditors can verify the accuracy of financial and operational data without the possibility of tampering. This can significantly reduce the time and cost associated with audit processes and increase their reliability. The immutability of blockchain is more than just a technical feature; it is a fundamental characteristic that ensures data integrity, enhances security, and fosters trust among users. By providing a secure, verifiable, and permanent record of transactions, blockchain immutability becomes an essential tool for a wide range of applications, offering significant benefits over traditional systems in terms of transparency, security, and efficiency.

Blockchain technology is revolutionizing supply chain management by offering a transparent, unalterable record of the entire supply chain from production to delivery. This capability significantly enhances traceability, efficiency, and accountability within supply chain operations, providing numerous benefits across various industries.

The application of blockchain in supply chain management allows for real-time tracking of goods as they move from origin to destination. Each transaction associated with the item's journey is recorded on a decentralized ledger, providing a permanent history of the product's path. This level of detail ensures that all stakeholders, from manufacturers to end consumers, can trace the product's journey at any point in time. Such traceability is particularly valuable in industries like pharmaceuticals, where verifying the authenticity of drugs and their components is critical, or in the food industry, where consumers increasingly demand to know the origins and handling of the food they consume.

By automating and recording every transaction upon execution, blockchain reduces the need for manual tracking and eliminates common inefficiencies such as data entry errors and delays in paperwork. For instance, blockchain can streamline processes like customs clearances and payment approvals, which traditionally require considerable time and paperwork. This automation speeds up the entire supply chain, allowing goods to flow more quickly and smoothly from producers to consumers. It also reduces operational costs by cutting down on the labor and time required to track and verify shipments.

Blockchain's immutability plays a crucial role in enhancing accountability within supply chains. Since each record is permanent and visible to all participants, it is nearly impossible to alter data unilaterally. This transparency helps reduce fraud and errors because every part of the chain can be audited to ensure compliance with regulations and standards. For example, in the case of ethical sourcing and fair trade practices, blockchain can help verify that goods have been produced and handled according to agreed-upon ethical and environmental standards, reassuring consumers and regulators alike.

Various implementations of blockchain in supply chain management are already underway. For instance, major retailers and food suppliers use blockchain to track produce from farms to stores, ensuring that all food items are fresh and handled properly. Similarly, luxury goods manufacturers deploy blockchain to certify the authenticity of their products, preventing counterfeiting and unauthorized sales channels.

Looking ahead, the integration of blockchain in supply chain management is poised to grow further as businesses continue to recognize its potential to transform traditional practices. The technology not only fosters greater operational transparency but also builds consumer trust by ensuring product authenticity and ethical compliance. As more sectors adopt blockchain for supply chain management, it is expected to drive more sustainable, responsive, and consumer-oriented business models, reshaping how global trade and logistics are conducted in the digital age.

Blockchain technology is increasingly being viewed as a transformative solution for managing and securing medical records within the healthcare sector. By storing medical records on a blockchain, both the security of sensitive data and the control over this data are significantly enhanced for patients and healthcare providers alike.

One of the most compelling advantages of using blockchain for medical records is the enhanced security it provides. Blockchain's structure—where data is decentralized and spread across multiple nodes—makes it extremely difficult for hackers to compromise the integrity of the data. Each block of data is encrypted and linked to the previous block, creating a secure chain that ensures no single point of failure. This level of security is crucial in healthcare, where patients' medical records often contain sensitive information that must be protected from unauthorized access and breaches. Blockchain technology empowers patients by giving them control over their medical records. Patients can have their health data stored on a blockchain with private keys that only they possess, allowing them to control who accesses their information. This is a significant shift from traditional healthcare information systems, where patients have little insight into who views their records. With blockchain, patients can grant or revoke access to their medical data as needed, enhancing their privacy and autonomy over personal health information.

The immutable nature of blockchain ensures that once information is entered, it cannot be altered without consensus from the network, thereby maintaining the accuracy of the medical records. This feature is particularly important in healthcare, where the accuracy of medical information is paramount. Healthcare providers benefit from having access to reliable and unalterable medical histories, which can significantly enhance the quality of care provided.

Blockchain facilitates the accessibility of medical records. Healthcare providers can quickly and securely access patient data from the blockchain, provided they have authorization from the patient. This accessibility can be crucial in emergency situations where immediate access to a patient's medical history could influence the course of treatment and significantly affect outcomes. Another significant advantage of using blockchain in healthcare is the potential for increased interoperability between different healthcare systems. Currently, medical data is often siloed within different healthcare institutions and systems, making it difficult to share information efficiently. Blockchain can serve as a universal ledger on which all healthcare providers operate, allowing for seamless exchange and access to medical data across various platforms and geographies without compromising security.

While the benefits are substantial, there are also challenges to implementing blockchain for medical records. These include the scale of data migration from existing systems to a blockchain, ensuring compliance with health data regulations such as HIPAA in the U.S., and addressing concerns around the scalability and speed of blockchain transactions. Despite these challenges, the potential benefits of applying blockchain technology in healthcare continue to drive interest and experimentation in this area.

Blockchain technology holds the promise of revolutionizing the management of medical records by enhancing security, improving data accessibility, and granting patients greater control over their personal information. As the technology matures and solutions to current challenges are developed, blockchain could significantly impact how healthcare data is managed globally, leading to more coordinated, efficient, and patient-centered healthcare systems. Blockchain technology extends far beyond the realm of cryptocurrencies, offering transformative potential for the broader financial services sector. Its capabilities to streamline payments, reduce fraud, and lower operational costs represent a significant shift in how financial transactions and contracts are managed and executed.

One of the most direct applications of blockchain in financial services is in streamlining payment systems. Blockchain enables faster, more secure, and more efficient payment processing than traditional banking systems by eliminating the need for intermediaries like banks and payment processors. Transactions on a blockchain can occur directly between parties, significantly reducing the time it takes to settle payments—from days to mere minutes or even seconds. This efficiency not only improves liquidity but also enhances the user experience by providing faster access to funds, which is particularly beneficial in international trade where payment delays are common. Blockchain's decentralized and transparent nature makes it an excellent tool for reducing fraud in financial transactions. Each transaction on a blockchain is recorded on a ledger that is immutable and visible to all network participants, making any attempt at fraud easy to detect. This transparency helps prevent common fraudulent practices such as double spending, where an individual attempts to initiate more than one transaction using the same funds. Moreover, the use of cryptographic techniques ensures that all transactions are securely encrypted, thus safeguarding against hacking and unauthorized access.

Blockchain can significantly reduce costs associated with financial transactions. By cutting out intermediaries and the associated fees, blockchain lowers the cost of transactions for both financial institutions and their customers. Additionally, blockchain's capability to automate various processes through smart contracts further reduces administrative and operational expenses. Smart contracts are self-executing contracts with the terms of the agreement between buyer and seller being directly written into lines of code. These contracts automatically execute and enforce themselves based on these coded terms when certain conditions are met, thereby eliminating the need for manual processing, which is often labor-intensive and costly.

The application of smart contracts in financial services extends beyond simple transactions. They can be used for more complex financial instruments and services such as loans, insurance, and derivatives. For example, in the insurance industry, smart contracts can automatically process claims and disburse payments if the encoded conditions are met, such as verified damage in an insured property due to natural disasters. This automation not only speeds up the processing of claims but also reduces the possibility of disputes and the potential for fraud. While blockchain offers numerous benefits, there are challenges to its broader adoption within the financial services sector. These include scalability issues, as some blockchain networks can handle only a limited number of transactions per second compared to traditional payment networks. There are also regulatory challenges, as the global financial regulatory environment is complex and varies significantly between jurisdictions.

Despite these challenges, the potential of blockchain in financial services continues to attract significant interest and investment from both startups and established financial institutions. As the technology evolves and solutions to these challenges are developed, blockchain is expected to play an increasingly central role in reshaping the financial services landscape, making it more efficient, secure, and inclusive.

Blockchain technology has the potential to fundamentally transform voting systems around the world, providing a secure, transparent, and tamper-proof method for casting and recording votes. This innovative application could greatly reduce instances of electoral fraud and possibly increase voter turnout by making the voting process more accessible and trustworthy. The cornerstone of blockchain technology is its security. By leveraging blockchain, each vote can be encrypted and recorded as a unique transaction on a distributed ledger. This record is then verified and sealed by consensus algorithms, ensuring that no single entity can alter it post-submission without detection. This level of security not only prevents potential tampering but also builds trust in the electoral process, as voters can be confident that their votes are accurately counted and remain unchanged.

Transparency is another significant advantage offered by blockchain-based voting systems. While ensuring voter anonymity, blockchain allows every transaction, or vote, to be traceable, verifiable, and auditable by authorized parties without revealing the voter's identity. This open verification process is crucial for maintaining the integrity of the election, as it ensures that all stakeholders can trust the results as being fair and free of manipulation. Moreover, in contentious elections, the blockchain provides an immutable audit trail that can be referenced to address any concerns about the voting results.

Blockchain technology could also increase voter turnout by simplifying the voting process and making it more accessible. Traditional voting methods often require physical presence at voting stations, which can be a barrier for people living in remote areas, those with disabilities, or those who cannot take time off work. A blockchain-based voting system can enable secure and verifiable voting via smartphones or computers, allowing more people to participate in the electoral process from the comfort of their homes or from any location with internet access. This convenience could encourage higher participation rates, especially among younger and technologically savvy demographics.

One of the most critical benefits of implementing blockchain in voting systems is the potential reduction in electoral fraud. The decentralized nature of blockchain means that manipulating the voting process would require altering multiple copies of the ledger simultaneously, a task that is virtually impossible without detection. This can significantly decrease the chances of both small-scale fraud, such as double voting, and large-scale fraud, such as tampering with or deleting votes, which can occur in less secure voting systems.

Despite these benefits, the adoption of blockchain in voting systems is not without challenges. Technical issues such as scalability, voter privacy, and security of voting devices must be addressed to fully realize the potential of blockchain-based voting. Additionally, there are significant regulatory and legal hurdles to overcome, as well as the need for public education and acceptance of this new approach to voting. As technology and societal attitudes continue to evolve, blockchain-based voting systems represent a promising advancement in electoral processes. By addressing the existing challenges and continuing to develop the technology's capabilities, blockchain could soon provide a globally trusted platform for conducting elections that are not only more secure and transparent but also more inclusive and accessible. This shift has the potential to transform democratic processes, reinforcing the foundations of trust and participation that are vital to effective governance.

Blockchain technology is increasingly being recognized for its potential to contribute significantly to environmental sustainability. By offering transparent records of energy usage and carbon emissions, blockchain can play a crucial role in enhancing environmental accountability and promoting sustainable practices across various industries.

The immutable and transparent nature of blockchain provides an ideal platform for recording and verifying environmental data. For instance, companies can use blockchain to maintain accessible, unalterable records of their carbon emissions and other environmental impacts. This transparency not only helps regulatory bodies ensure that businesses adhere to environmental standards, but it also allows companies to demonstrate their commitment to sustainability to consumers and investors.

Blockchain can facilitate the implementation of more sustainable practices by providing a reliable and efficient method for tracking the environmental impacts of specific actions and policies. For example, a company could use blockchain to monitor the lifecycle environmental impact of its products from raw material extraction through manufacturing, distribution, and disposal. This level of traceability can help identify opportunities for reducing environmental footprints and optimizing resource use, such as switching to renewable energy sources or recycling materials. Blockchain also offers significant advantages for carbon credit trading. By tokenizing carbon credits, blockchain can ensure that each credit is only used once and provide a transparent pathway from the credit's issuance to its retirement. This can help prevent fraud in the carbon market, making carbon trading more reliable and effective as a tool for reducing global emissions. Platforms leveraging blockchain for carbon trading can support the enforcement of caps on emissions and foster a real market price for carbon, encouraging polluters to adopt cleaner technologies.

In the energy sector, blockchain is being utilized to create decentralized platforms that allow for more efficient management and distribution of renewable energy. For instance, blockchain can enable peer-to-peer energy trading, allowing households with solar panels to sell excess electricity directly to neighbors, bypassing traditional utility companies. This not only makes renewable energy more accessible but also encourages its adoption by making it more economically viable for more people. Blockchain can simplify environmental compliance and reporting processes. By securely recording emissions data and other environmental impacts, blockchain makes it easier for companies to produce accurate environmental reports that comply with regulations. This can also streamline the audit processes by providing auditors with easily accessible and verifiable environmental data, reducing the time and cost associated with compliance.

Despite these potential benefits, the application of blockchain in environmental sustainability faces challenges, including technological limitations, regulatory uncertainties, and the need for significant energy to run blockchain systems themselves. Addressing these challenges requires continuous technological improvements, clearer regulatory frameworks, and the development of more energy-efficient blockchain systems. As these issues are addressed, blockchain's role in promoting environmental sustainability is likely to grow, offering more robust and innovative solutions for tracking, verifying, and encouraging environmentally responsible behaviors. This could significantly contribute to global sustainability efforts, providing a more transparent, accountable, and efficient approach to environmental management.

Blockchain technology holds the promise of transforming industries by enabling greater security, transparency, and efficiency. However, realizing its full potential will require overcoming significant challenges, including scalability, energy consumption, and regulatory acceptance. Despite these hurdles, blockchain's foundational principles offer a blueprint for a more transparent, secure, and equitable digital future. This technology is increasingly recognized for its potential to address some of the world's most pressing challenges, aligning closely with Environmental, Social, and Governance (ESG) objectives. By leveraging its inherent characteristics of transparency, security, and immutability, blockchain initiatives are being developed to foster sustainability, promote social equity, and enhance governance across the globe.

In the realm of renewable energy, blockchain platforms are transforming how energy is traded, creating decentralized networks that facilitate direct transactions between producers and consumers of renewable energy. This model significantly promotes the use of clean energy sources by bypassing traditional power grids and utility providers, allowing for a more efficient and transparent exchange of energy. Platforms such as WePower are pioneering this space by enabling renewable energy producers to raise capital through the issuance of tradable energy tokens. These tokens represent a certain amount of energy production and can be purchased by consumers directly. This not only provides producers with the upfront capital needed for expansion but also empowers consumers to directly invest in and consume green energy, thereby fostering a more sustainable energy ecosystem and contributing to the reduction of overall carbon footprints.

Blockchain is making significant strides in enhancing supply chain transparency. Its ability to provide a transparent and immutable record of transactions makes it an ideal technology for tracking the entire lifecycle of a product from raw material sourcing to final delivery. This level of transparency ensures that companies can verify and guarantee that their products are sustainably sourced and ethically produced. For instance, IBM's Food Trust initiative utilizes blockchain to trace the origin and journey of food products. By doing so, it not only reduces waste by improving logistics and eliminating inefficiencies but also ensures food safety and strengthens consumer trust. Additionally, it supports responsible environmental practices by enabling consumers and companies to make more informed decisions based on the ecological impact of their purchases.

These applications of blockchain in environmental sustainability demonstrate the technology's potential not only to support existing systems but also to innovate new solutions that address critical challenges. By aligning blockchain technology with sustainability goals, it becomes a powerful tool for companies committed to reducing their environmental impact and for consumers who are increasingly demanding transparency and responsibility from the products they consume. Through initiatives like renewable energy trading and enhanced supply chain visibility, blockchain is helping pave the way towards a more sustainable and environmentally conscious global economy.

Blockchain technology is increasingly recognized as a powerful tool for promoting social equity, primarily through two critical avenues: enhancing financial inclusion and providing robust identity verification solutions. These applications are pivotal in addressing systemic barriers and fostering greater inclusivity within the global economy.

Blockchain technology is at the forefront of efforts to enhance financial inclusion globally. A significant portion of the world's population remains unbanked or underbanked, often due to geographic isolation, lack of official documentation, or insufficient credit history. Traditional banking infrastructures fail to serve these populations effectively, but blockchain introduces innovative solutions to bridge this gap. Through cryptocurrencies and mobile blockchain wallets, blockchain technology offers practical alternatives to conventional financial services. These tools enable individuals in remote or economically marginalized communities to engage with the global economy more fully. For example, blockchain allows for the receipt of international remittances at reduced costs, facilitates access to crucial financial services like savings accounts and loans, and provides a degree of financial autonomy that was previously unattainable for many.

The democratization of access to financial services via blockchain not only empowers individuals economically but also supports broader economic empowerment. It helps level the playing field, offering fairer access to financial resources and opportunities which, in turn, contributes to reducing the global financial divide.

In addition to financial inclusion, blockchain plays a critical role in identity verification, particularly benefiting refugees and individuals in developing nations. For many in these groups, proving one's identity is a formidable barrier to accessing essential services such as healthcare, banking, and education. Blockchain-based identity solutions provide a secure, immutable, and user-centric method for managing and verifying personal identities. Initiatives like ID2020 are pioneering the use of digital identities that offer safe, portable, and universally recognized identification forms. These digital IDs are secured on the blockchain, ensuring they remain tamper-proof and accessible, irrespective of geographical location or political instability. Such technology is transformative, providing not only security but also enhanced access to vital services that underpin personal and economic development.

These blockchain-driven initiatives are instrumental in fostering social equity. They provide critical tools for financial inclusion and secure identity verification, empowering marginalized or underserved groups and bridging significant gaps in access to economic resources and services. The impact of these technologies extends far beyond individual benefits. They contribute to the overarching goals of inclusive growth and equitable access to opportunities, which are crucial for the stability and progress of societies worldwide.

By leveraging blockchain for these purposes, we can address some of the most persistent challenges in social equity, reducing disparities and promoting a more inclusive global community. This technology empowers individuals, enhances communities, and redefines participation in the global economy, ensuring that the benefits of technological advancements are shared broadly and equitably.

Blockchain technology is increasingly recognized for its potential to enhance governance and promote ethical practices across various sectors. Its capacity to provide a transparent and immutable record of transactions makes it a powerful tool for combating corruption, particularly in sensitive areas like public procurement and international aid. For instance, organizations such as Transparency International are exploring blockchain's potential to track and report corrupt activities, thereby enhancing governance and accountability. This use of blockchain can lead to significant improvements in how transactions and interactions are monitored, ensuring that all activities are conducted above board and can be audited by the public or relevant authorities.

In addition to anti-corruption measures, blockchain's smart contracts offer revolutionary possibilities for ensuring ethical governance. These contracts are self-executing, with the terms of the agreement directly written into code. They automatically enforce themselves when certain conditions are met, reducing the need for intermediaries and decreasing the potential for disputes. For example, in the context of environmental, social, and governance (ESG) commitments, smart contracts can be designed to release funds for sustainability projects only after specific environmental milestones have been reached. This not only ensures that funds are used as intended but also promotes accountability and encourages the completion of project goals.

Blockchain facilitates the tokenization of environmental assets, such as carbon credits or biodiversity offsets. This process allows these assets to be represented by digital tokens that can be traded on blockchain platforms. Organizations like Verra and the Carbon Trade Exchange are leveraging blockchain to improve the transparency and efficiency of carbon credit markets. Through blockchain, environmental assets can be accurately quantified, tracked, and traded in a transparent manner, ensuring that each credit's impact is real, measurable, and verifiable. This not only helps regulate and stimulate the market for environmental assets but also supports global efforts in environmental conservation.

The integration of blockchain into governance and ethical practices provides a robust framework for enhancing transparency, accountability, and efficiency. By harnessing blockchain's capabilities, sectors involved in public administration, international aid, and environmental management can achieve higher standards of ethical governance, ultimately leading to more just and sustainable outcomes. As blockchain technology continues to evolve and be adopted, its role in shaping ethical and transparent governance frameworks looks set to grow, potentially transforming how institutions and industries manage their operations and uphold their responsibilities to stakeholders and the broader community. These blockchain initiatives exemplify the technology's potential to support and advance ESG objectives. By addressing environmental sustainability, promoting social equity, and enhancing governance and ethical practices, blockchain is proving to be a valuable tool in the quest for a more sustainable, equitable, and responsibly governed world. As these initiatives continue to develop and scale, the alignment of blockchain technology with ESG goals could drive significant progress in tackling global challenges.

Chapter 2: Blockchain as a Tool for Transformative Social Innovation

In the evolving discourse around blockchain technology, much attention is given to its financial implications—often overshadowing its profound capacity for social innovation within Environmental, Social, and Governance (ESG) frameworks. As we delve deeper into blockchain's role in these areas, we find it is not just a foundational technology for economic activities but a pivotal enabler of transformative social change. This section explores how blockchain acts as a lever for social betterment, promoting sustainability, equity, and ethical governance through a series of insightful case studies and evaluations.

Decentralized Finance, commonly known as DeFi, is transforming the landscape of financial services by leveraging blockchain technology to provide a wide range of services without the traditional banking infrastructure. This shift toward decentralization is particularly impactful for those who have historically been underserved by conventional financial systems, such as individuals in remote or economically disadvantaged areas.

DeFi platforms operate on the premise that access to financial services should not be contingent on geographic location or access to a physical bank. Instead, they utilize blockchain technology to create financial systems where transactions are executed securely and transparently on a decentralized ledger. This allows anyone with an internet connection to access services such as loans, savings accounts, insurance, and asset trading, directly from their digital devices.

The implications of this are profound, especially for those in underserved regions. By removing the barriers to entry typically associated with traditional banking—such as account minimums, credit checks, and physical infrastructure—DeFi opens up financial opportunities to a much larger population. For example, small-scale entrepreneurs in developing countries can access microloans to start or expand their businesses without the need for a bank account or credit history, which might be difficult to establish in areas without comprehensive financial services.

DeFi can provide more favorable terms for financial services by eliminating the middlemen and the associated costs. This can result in lower fees for transfers and transactions, higher interest rates on savings accounts, and more affordable premiums for insurance. The cost savings are achieved because the blockchain technology that underpins DeFi platforms automates many of the processes that would typically require human oversight and thus, administrative costs in traditional banking. DeFi also introduces a higher level of transparency that is not usually found in conventional finance. Every transaction on a DeFi platform is recorded on the blockchain, making it publicly verifiable by anyone at any time. This transparency ensures fairness and can build trust among users who might be skeptical of or unfamiliar with traditional financial systems.

While DeFi has the potential to democratize access to financial services radically, it also presents challenges that need to be addressed to ensure its long-term sustainability and safety. These include the risk of technical glitches, the need for improved security protocols to prevent fraud, and the establishment of regulatory frameworks to protect users without stifling innovation. As DeFi continues to evolve, it could significantly alter how financial services are delivered worldwide. By empowering the underserved with tools for economic inclusion, DeFi not only has the potential to level the financial playing field but also to foster broader economic development in areas that traditional finance has failed to reach.

In Sub-Saharan Africa, a region where access to traditional banking services is often limited, particularly in rural areas, a blockchain-based platform is pioneering changes in the way micro-lending is conducted. This innovative approach to microfinance is empowering small entrepreneurs who previously found themselves excluded from the conventional financial system due to geographic and economic barriers.

The platform harnesses blockchain technology to facilitate the disbursement and repayment of small loans directly through mobile devices. This method is highly advantageous in a region with high mobile phone penetration but low banking infrastructure. Entrepreneurs in these areas can now apply for and receive micro-loans without the need for a physical bank account, bridging a significant gap in financial services.

One of the key features of this blockchain-based micro-lending platform is the transparency it brings to financial transactions. Each loan disbursed and each repayment made is recorded on a decentralized and immutable ledger. This not only ensures that records cannot be altered fraudulently but also allows lenders—whether they are local microfinance institutions or international investors—to see the real-time impact of their contributions. They can track when loans are disbursed and see how borrowers are using the funds to grow their businesses, invest in their communities, or improve their living conditions.

This level of transparency has significantly increased trust in the micro-lending process. Lenders have more confidence that their funds are being used as intended, which in turn encourages them to invest more. Furthermore, the blockchain platform also reduces the costs and complexities associated with managing micro-loans, which traditionally involved extensive paperwork and administrative overhead. By cutting down these costs, the platform ensures that a larger portion of the funds can directly benefit the borrowers, making the lending process more efficient and impactful.

The positive impact of this blockchain-enabled micro-lending is evident in the cycle of investment and growth it creates. As small entrepreneurs gain access to credit, they are able to invest in their businesses—buying equipment, hiring staff, or expanding their operations. This not only boosts their own economic standing but also has a multiplier effect on the local economy. More successful businesses create more jobs, increase household incomes, and stimulate economic activity in the region. The success of these small enterprises often leads to increased repayment rates, as borrowers are able to return their loans from the profits of their expanded businesses. High repayment rates further boost lender confidence, attracting more investments into the platform and enabling more loans to be disbursed.

The introduction of blockchain technology into micro-lending in Sub-Saharan Africa is a prime example of how innovative digital solutions can be applied to long-standing challenges. By providing a secure, transparent, and accessible platform for financial transactions, blockchain is not only transforming the landscape of microfinance but is also helping drive economic development and empowerment at the grassroots level. This case study underscores the significant potential of technology to foster financial inclusion and stimulate socio-economic growth in regions most in need of such transformation.

Blockchain technology is increasingly being recognized as a robust solution to the pervasive issues of land ownership disputes in many developing countries. These disputes are frequently exacerbated by inadequate record-keeping systems and widespread corruption in land registry offices. The adoption of blockchain technology in this sector could revolutionize how land registries are maintained, by ensuring transparency, security, and immutability in land ownership records.

In regions where land ownership disputes are common, the traditional systems for recording land transactions are often outdated, prone to manipulation, and can be easily corrupted. Records may be incomplete or inaccessible, and fraudulent claims over land are not uncommon. This situation not only leads to legal disputes but also undermines economic development, as unclear land ownership can deter investment and complicate the use of land as collateral for loans.

Blockchain technology introduces a fundamentally different approach to land registry by utilizing its immutable ledger to maintain a clear, accurate, and permanent record of land ownership. Once a land transaction is recorded on a blockchain, it cannot be altered or deleted. This immutability is enforced through cryptographic hashing, which secures each block of data and chains it to the preceding block, making unauthorized changes virtually impossible without detection across the entire network.

The transparent nature of blockchain also means that every transaction is visible to all parties involved, ensuring that changes in land ownership are openly verified and traceable back to their origins. This level of transparency significantly reduces the potential for fraud, as any illicit attempts to alter the ledger would be immediately apparent to other users. Moreover, this openness helps build trust among stakeholders, including landowners, potential buyers, financial institutions, and government authorities.

Implementing blockchain for land registries not only resolves the issues of security and transparency but also enhances accessibility. Land records stored on a blockchain can be accessed by any authorized user from anywhere, without the need for physical travel to local registry offices. This ease of access is particularly beneficial in remote areas, where traditional methods of record-keeping can be a significant barrier to land management and investment. Blockchain can streamline the process of land transactions, reducing the time and cost associated with land registration and transfer. Smart contracts, which are self-executing contracts with the terms of the agreement directly written into code, can automate many of the legal and administrative procedures involved in land dealings. For instance, a smart contract could automatically transfer ownership and update the registry as soon as payment is verified, all without the need for manual processing.

While the potential benefits of blockchain in land registry are clear, challenges such as technological adoption, legal integration, and the initial digitization of existing records must be addressed. Governments and stakeholders must collaborate to develop regulatory frameworks that support the use of blockchain technology while ensuring that it complements existing legal systems.

Blockchain technology presents a compelling solution to the challenges of land registry in developing countries. By providing a secure, transparent, and immutable record of land ownership, blockchain can help resolve disputes, reduce corruption, and facilitate clearer and more accessible land ownership. This, in turn, can lead to greater economic stability and development by making land a more reliable asset for investment and development. In Honduras, a country plagued by inefficiencies and corruption within its land registration system, the implementation of a blockchain-based system for managing land titles marked a significant turning point. After years of public frustration, where citizens faced rampant illegal land grabs and ambiguous ownership records, the new blockchain initiative was introduced to overhaul and improve the process.

Traditional land registry system in Honduras was notorious for its susceptibility to manipulation and fraud. Records could be easily altered, and land titles were often illegally modified or duplicated, leading to widespread disputes over land ownership. This unreliable system not only fueled corruption but also deterred investment in the real estate sector, as potential buyers and developers were understandably wary of the risks associated with unclear land titles.

The introduction of a blockchain-based system transformed the landscape of land registration in Honduras by leveraging the technology's core characteristics of immutability and transparency. Once a land transaction is recorded on the blockchain, it is secured by cryptographic means and cannot be altered or deleted. This immutability ensures that every transaction in the registry remains permanent and unchangeable, effectively eliminating the possibility for fraud that was rampant under the old system. Transparency provided by blockchain technology means that all records are accessible to authorized users, providing a clear, auditable trail of ownership history that is open and verifiable. This aspect of the technology has restored trust in the land registration process, as every change in ownership is transparently recorded and easily traceable. The impact of the blockchain initiative in Honduras has been profound. Illegal land grabs, which were once a common occurrence due to the ease of manipulating paper-based records, have significantly decreased. The security features of blockchain have deterred fraudulent activities by making unauthorized alterations practically impossible. As a result, the incidence of land disputes has reduced, leading to greater stability and security in land ownership.

The clarity and reliability of land titles managed on the blockchain have boosted confidence among investors and the general public. The real estate sector, in particular, has seen a notable increase in activity as more people are willing to buy and sell property. The assurance that land titles are secure and disputes are less likely encourages investment, driving economic growth and development in the region. Property values have stabilized, and foreign investors, previously deterred by the risk of title fraud, are showing renewed interest in the Honduran real estate market.

The success of the blockchain land title initiative in Honduras serves as a compelling case study for other countries facing similar challenges with land registration. It illustrates the potential of blockchain technology to address systemic issues in public administration by enhancing security, transparency, and efficiency. As more countries look to modernize their land registry systems, the example set by Honduras offers valuable insights into the transformative impact that blockchain can have on governance and economic development.

For refugees and displaced individuals, the lack of official identification presents a significant barrier to accessing essential services such as healthcare, education, and banking. Without recognized identification, these individuals often find themselves excluded from the formal economy, unable to receive legal employment, open bank accounts, secure housing, or access healthcare and educational facilities. Blockchain technology, with its inherent security, immutability, and portability, offers a transformative solution for creating digital identities that can help overcome these challenges. Blockchain's secure nature stems from its decentralized and cryptographic structure, ensuring that any data stored on it cannot be altered or forged. This is particularly crucial for digital identities, as the information must be protected from unauthorized access and tampering. For refugees, who may not have access to traditional forms of ID due to displacement or the loss of documents during migration, a blockchain-based digital identity provides a secure and verifiable alternative that is resistant to fraud and identity theft.

One of the most significant advantages of blockchain-based digital identities is their portability. Unlike physical documents, which can be lost or destroyed, digital identities on the blockchain can be accessed anywhere and anytime, provided there is internet access. This portability is crucial for refugees and displaced individuals who often move across borders. A blockchain identity can follow them wherever they go, eliminating the need to start the identification process anew with each relocation.

With a secure and portable digital identity, refugees can prove their identity and access essential services more easily. For example, in healthcare, blockchain identities can help medical professionals access a refugee's medical records quickly, ensuring timely and appropriate treatment. In education, these identities can facilitate the enrollment process in schools by providing verifiable data on the educational background of displaced children, helping to integrate them into the education system of their host countries.

In banking and financial services, blockchain can provide the unbanked or underbanked—common among refugee populations—with the means to open bank accounts, receive and make payments, and access other financial services that are often critical for starting over in a new country. The ability to engage financially helps not only in day-to-day survival but also in building and maintaining livelihoods in new environments.

For blockchain-based digital identities to be fully effective, however, there must be legal recognition and integration into existing systems by governments and international organizations. This involves regulatory frameworks that acknowledge digital identities as valid forms of identification. It also requires collaboration between technology providers, non-governmental organizations, and government bodies to ensure these digital solutions meet the practical needs of refugees and align with global standards for privacy and data protection.

Blockchain technology offers a promising pathway to inclusivity for refugees and displaced individuals through secure, immutable, and portable digital identities. These identities can facilitate access to vital services, contributing significantly to the integration and empowerment of some of the world's most vulnerable populations. As this technology continues to evolve and gain acceptance, it has the potential to play a crucial role in addressing the complex challenges associated with identity verification in humanitarian contexts.

A pioneering project that utilizes blockchain technology to provide digital identities for refugees is transforming the way displaced individuals integrate into new communities. Many refugees, in the chaos of fleeing their home countries, lose crucial documents like passports and birth certificates. This loss creates significant barriers as these individuals struggle to prove their identity, which is essential for accessing vital services and opportunities in new environments. The blockchain-based digital identity initiative addresses this challenge by creating secure, immutable, and universally recognized digital IDs. These digital IDs are recorded on a blockchain ledger, ensuring that the information is permanent and unchangeable. Including critical identification and personal data encrypted for security, these IDs allow refugees to prove their identity without traditional paperwork. They can be accessed through biometric data or unique identifiers, making them both user-friendly and secure against fraud or theft.

The acceptance of these digital IDs by a range of service providers is crucial for their effectiveness. Partner organizations, including banks, healthcare providers, educational institutions, and government services, recognize these blockchain IDs as valid forms of identification. This recognition enables refugees to engage in a variety of essential activities: they can open bank accounts, receive medical care, enroll in schools, and access government assistance, all of which are critical for their survival and integration into new environments.

For example, in healthcare, refugees can access services swiftly and smoothly, with medical providers able to verify identities and medical histories quickly and accurately. In the financial sector, these IDs enable refugees to carry out financial transactions, crucial for managing remittances, savings, or even starting small businesses. Furthermore, having reliable identification helps refugees find employment, rent housing, and participate more fully in their new communities, enhancing both their well-being and that of the host communities. Despite its successes, the project faces challenges such as ensuring widespread acceptance of blockchain IDs, maintaining robust data protection to secure privacy, and overcoming logistical and technological hurdles, especially in under-resourced areas. Future progress will depend on continued collaboration among technology developers, humanitarian organizations, government bodies, and the private sector.

This case study of providing blockchain-based digital identities to refugees illustrates how technology can address complex social issues effectively. By restoring identities to those who have lost everything, blockchain technology not only facilitates access to essential services but also supports broader goals of dignity, security, and integration for some of the world's most vulnerable populations. This innovative use of technology sets a precedent for other scenarios where identity verification poses a significant challenge, showcasing the potential of blockchain to drive social good.

Evaluating the impact of blockchain initiatives is crucial for understanding their effectiveness and ensuring their continuous improvement. To thoroughly assess these initiatives, both quantitative metrics and qualitative assessments are employed, providing a comprehensive overview of outcomes. Quantitative data is vital as it offers concrete evidence of the initiatives' impacts. For example, tracking the number of individuals who gain access to financial services through blockchain platforms gives a clear indication of success in enhancing financial inclusion. Similarly, measuring the reduction in land ownership disputes and the efficiency of their resolution can demonstrate the effectiveness of blockchain in land registry systems. Additionally, for projects aimed at providing digital identities to refugees, counting the number of identities issued and used to access services provides quantitative proof of progress.

Quantitative metrics only tell part of the story. Qualitative assessments add depth to the evaluation by capturing community and stakeholder feedback about their experiences with the blockchain services. Through interviews, focus groups, and surveys, insights about user satisfaction, system reliability, and user-friendliness are gathered. These assessments help determine whether the blockchain solutions are meeting the needs of users and highlight any areas needing improvement.

Qualitative data plays a crucial role in evaluating the long-term sustainability of the blockchain solutions. It helps understand whether the solutions are culturally acceptable, economically viable, and environmentally sustainable. Feedback from stakeholders can reveal whether the blockchain initiatives are effectively integrating into users' daily lives and whether they are likely to continue using these services in the future.

By combining quantitative and qualitative methods, a more nuanced understanding of the blockchain initiatives' effectiveness is achieved. While quantitative data provides the hard numbers to demonstrate impact, qualitative insights offer the context and user experiences behind these numbers. For instance, even if quantitative data shows a high number of processed land titles through a blockchain system, qualitative feedback may indicate whether landowners genuinely feel more secure about their ownership status and perceive the system as transparent and fair. Similarly, while the number of digital identities issued is important, understanding how these identities have helped refugees access services and integrate into communities is equally crucial. This comprehensive approach to evaluation not only measures the extent of success but also identifies areas for improvement, ensuring that blockchain technology continues to evolve in ways that meet user needs and maximize its transformative potential across various sectors.

While blockchain presents numerous opportunities for social innovation, it also faces challenges. Scalability, energy consumption, and the need for widespread technological literacy are significant hurdles. Additionally, regulatory frameworks must evolve to support ethical innovation while ensuring these technologies do not exacerbate existing social inequalities.

As we look to the future, the intersection of blockchain with other cutting-edge technologies like artificial intelligence and the Internet of Things promises to further expand its capabilities. Smart contracts could automate welfare distributions in a transparent way, and IoT devices could provide real-time data to blockchain networks, enhancing decision-making processes in smart cities. Through these initiatives and the continued development of blockchain technology, we see a powerful tool for achieving the ESG goals. The case studies highlighted in this section provide a snapshot of the potential for blockchain to drive substantial social change, marking just the beginning of its application in creating a more equitable and sustainable world.

Blockchain technology is reshaping not only the financial sector but also emerging as a pivotal tool for addressing complex social challenges within the Environmental, Social, and Governance (ESG) framework. This section delves into how blockchain serves as a catalyst for social change, emphasizing its role through various impactful case studies that highlight its potential to enhance sustainability and ethical governance.

Decentralized Finance (DeFi) represents a transformative shift in the financial landscape, leveraging blockchain technology to democratize access to financial services. Unlike traditional finance, DeFi operates without the need for centralized financial intermediaries such as banks, credit unions, or clearinghouses. Instead, it utilizes smart contracts on blockchains, particularly Ethereum, to execute financial transactions and offer services ranging from loans and savings to complex financial instruments like derivatives and insurance. This shift has profound implications, particularly for unbanked populations in remote or underserved regions who have traditionally been excluded from the formal financial system. For these individuals, access to financial services can be life-changing, enabling them to save securely, access credit, and insure against risks without the high fees or entry barriers imposed by conventional financial institutions.

DeFi platforms are inherently inclusive, requiring only a smartphone and internet access for participation. This accessibility is facilitated by user-friendly mobile interfaces that simplify the interaction with complex underlying blockchain technologies. Through these interfaces, users can perform a variety of financial transactions that were previously unavailable to them, such as sending and receiving money across borders at low costs, investing in diverse asset classes, and securing loans without the need for formal credit checks or collateral as typically required by traditional banks. DeFi is built on the principles of openness and transparency. Every transaction on a DeFi platform is recorded on a blockchain, visible to anyone, ensuring that all operations are transparent and auditable. This not only helps in building trust among users but also significantly reduces the possibility of fraud and corruption, issues that are prevalent in many traditional banking systems, especially in less regulated markets.

Economic empowerment through DeFi also comes from the opportunity it provides for users to participate in the governance of these platforms. Many DeFi projects have governance tokens that give holders voting rights in decisions regarding the development and operation of the platform. This feature not only incentivizes participation by allowing users to benefit directly from the success of the platform but also aligns the interests of the users and developers towards the common goal of creating a more efficient and inclusive financial ecosystem. While DeFi offers significant advantages, it also comes with challenges that need to be addressed. These include the high volatility of crypto assets used on these platforms, the technical knowledge required to safely navigate these spaces, and the regulatory uncertainty surrounding blockchain and cryptocurrency. Additionally, the risk of smart contract vulnerabilities and the lack of insurance coverage for assets stored on DeFi platforms pose significant risks to users.

DeFi stands out as a powerful example of how blockchain can foster economic empowerment by breaking down the barriers to financial inclusion. By providing easy access to a range of financial services through decentralized platforms, DeFi has the potential to transform the economic realities for millions of people worldwide, particularly those in remote or underserved regions. As the technology matures and these platforms become more user-friendly and secure, the promise of DeFi in driving real-world adoption of blockchain for economic empowerment continues to grow.

In rural Southeast Asia, where access to traditional banking services has historically been limited, a DeFi platform is dramatically transforming the landscape of micro-lending. This platform leverages the power of decentralized finance to offer villagers who were previously excluded from the formal financial system an opportunity to engage in borrowing and lending directly through their mobile devices. This innovative approach is not only bridging the gap in financial inclusion but also catalyzing economic development within these communities.

The DeFi platform utilizes smart contracts on blockchain technology to facilitate the lending process. These smart contracts are programmed to automatically execute the terms of the loan when certain conditions are met, such as the borrower meeting repayment schedules or achieving specified business milestones. This automation significantly enhances the efficiency of the micro-lending process by eliminating the need for intermediaries such as banks or microfinance institutions, which often impose high transaction fees and lengthy processing times.

The use of blockchain ensures that all transactions are recorded in a transparent and immutable manner. This transparency is crucial as it allows both lenders and borrowers to track the flow of funds in real-time, ensuring that there is no mismanagement or diversion of the funds. For lenders, particularly those who might be based in urban centers or even overseas, this visibility builds confidence in the lending process, reassuring them that their funds are being used as intended.

The security features inherent in blockchain technology also play a vital role in minimizing the risks of fraud. With traditional micro-lending, there is often a risk of identity theft or fraudulent claims, which can lead to losses for both lenders and borrowers. However, on a blockchain-based DeFi platform, all parties are required to undergo rigorous verification processes, and all transactions are securely encrypted, significantly reducing the likelihood of fraud.

The impact of this DeFi-based micro-lending platform on rural communities in Southeast Asia has been profound. Small businesses and entrepreneurs, who previously had difficulty accessing capital due to the lack of collateral or credit history, can now receive loans to start or expand their businesses. This access to capital is vital for fostering entrepreneurship and stimulating economic activity within these communities. It enables local businesses to grow, creating jobs and improving the overall standard of living.

The success of these businesses often encourages more community members to participate in the DeFi platform, creating a virtuous cycle of investment and growth. As more individuals see the tangible benefits of accessible, transparent, and secure micro-lending, the more they are likely to engage with the platform, either as borrowers seeking to improve their economic prospects or as lenders looking to contribute to community development while earning returns on their investments.

The introduction of DeFi platforms in rural Southeast Asia is not just an exploration of new financial technology but a revolutionary step towards economic empowerment. By providing secure, transparent, and accessible micro-lending services, DeFi is helping to dismantle barriers to financial inclusion and paving the way for a more equitable distribution of economic resources and opportunities. Land ownership disputes are a pervasive problem in many developing regions, often causing significant social and economic issues. These disputes frequently arise from unreliable record-keeping systems and prevalent corruption in land registry offices. In such environments, records can be easily altered, lost, or manipulated, leading to uncertainty over land ownership that discourages investment and can lead to conflict. Blockchain technology provides a transformative solution to these problems with its inherent qualities of security and transparency.

Blockchain's primary advantage in land registry comes from its ability to maintain a secure, immutable ledger of transactions. Each land transaction recorded on a blockchain is timestamped and linked to previous transactions. Once a record is added to the blockchain, it cannot be altered or deleted, preventing unauthorized changes and fraud. This immutability is crucial for countries where tampering with land records has been a common practice to usurp land illegally.

Another significant benefit of using blockchain for land registries is enhanced transparency. Blockchain networks are designed to be transparent; all transactions recorded on the blockchain are visible to all parties involved and can be audited in real-time. This level of openness helps build trust among stakeholders, including landowners, potential buyers, and financial institutions, and can significantly reduce the time and cost associated with land transactions.

The use of blockchain also makes land records more accessible. Typically, accessing land records involves navigating bureaucratic processes that can be both time-consuming and costly. Blockchain platforms can allow multiple parties, including landowners, potential investors, and legal authorities, to access reliable and up-to-date land records online, thereby facilitating smoother and faster transactions.

By automating land registration processes through smart contracts, blockchain further reduces the human intervention required in transactions, thereby decreasing the potential for corruption. Smart contracts can automatically execute transactions based on predefined rules, such as the transfer of ownership once payment is verified. This not only speeds up the process but also minimizes the risk of corrupt practices that often occur in manual handling. Several countries have initiated blockchain projects to overhaul their land registry systems. For example, in Georgia, a blockchain land titling project has been implemented to secure land titles and streamline property transactions, providing a clear, auditable trail of title transfers. Similarly, in Sweden, blockchain trials have been conducted to explore the efficiencies it can bring to recording property transactions, reducing the time from several months to just a few days.

While blockchain presents clear advantages for land registry, there are challenges in its widespread adoption. These include the need for substantial technological infrastructure, the transition of existing records onto blockchain, and regulatory adjustments. Additionally, while blockchain can ensure the integrity of the records, the accuracy of the data initially entered into the system still needs to be ensured through rigorous checks and verification processes. Blockchain technology offers a robust solution for improving land registries in developing countries by providing secure, transparent, and immutable records. As more governments and organizations recognize its potential to resolve longstanding issues related to land ownership disputes, blockchain could become a standard technology in land registry systems worldwide, promoting greater economic development and social stability.

In Honduras, the adoption of a blockchain-based system to manage land records marks a significant advancement in addressing the country's chronic issues with land tenure security. The initiative has implemented blockchain technology to modernize the registry system, ensuring that every transaction related to land is recorded in a manner that is immutable and transparent. This transformation has had a profound effect on the overall integrity and reliability of land administration in the region.

The core strength of the blockchain system introduced in Honduras lies in its immutability. Once a land transaction is recorded on the blockchain, it becomes permanent and cannot be altered or tampered with. This feature is critical in a context where falsification of land records and illegal land grabs have been pervasive, often facilitated by corrupt practices within traditional registry systems. The blockchain's inherent resistance to modification ensures that each entry is preserved exactly as it was initially recorded, providing a durable and reliable record of ownership.

The transparency and security provided by blockchain technology have been instrumental in restoring trust in the property market in Honduras. Potential buyers and investors can now verify the history and legality of land titles independently and in real time, which has significantly reduced the risks associated with property transactions. This increased confidence has encouraged greater participation in the property market, fostering a more dynamic and stable real estate sector.

One of the most notable impacts of the blockchain land registry project in Honduras has been its effectiveness in curbing illegal land grabs. The clarity and accessibility of land ownership information make it much more difficult for illicit claims to be made without detection. As each transaction requires verification and consensus within the blockchain network before it is recorded, unauthorized alterations or fraudulent claims can be quickly identified and addressed. This robust level of security has deterred illegal activities, protecting legitimate landowners and reducing conflicts over land ownership. Despite its successes, the project faces challenges, particularly in terms of ensuring widespread adoption and understanding of the new technology among the population. Educational initiatives and outreach are necessary to help landowners and the general public understand how to access and use the blockchain system effectively. Moreover, continuous technological upgrades and maintenance are required to keep the system secure and operational.

The positive outcomes of the blockchain land registry in Honduras serve as a compelling case study for other countries grappling with similar issues. The project illustrates how technology can be leveraged to enhance legal frameworks and administrative processes in ways that promote transparency, reduce corruption, and provide tangible benefits to society. As more nations observe the benefits realized in Honduras, similar blockchain implementations may be considered elsewhere, potentially transforming land registry systems around the world.

The introduction of a blockchain-based land registry system in Honduras represents a groundbreaking step towards more secure and transparent land management practices. By ensuring the immutability of records and restoring trust in the property market, the project not only addresses local issues of land disputes and illegal grabs but also sets a benchmark for global best practices in land administration. Many refugees around the world face significant challenges in proving their identity. Without formal identification, accessing essential services such as healthcare, education, and banking becomes a formidable barrier. This situation often exacerbates the difficulties refugees face in attempting to rebuild their lives in new countries. Blockchain technology offers a robust solution by providing a secure method to create immutable and portable digital identities, which can be a transformative resource for refugees.

Blockchain technology enables the creation of digital identities that are secure, immutable, and portable. These digital IDs are stored on a decentralized network, ensuring they cannot be tampered with or erased. The immutability of blockchain means that once identity data is entered into the system, it remains secure and unchangeable without the consensus of the network. This feature is particularly crucial for refugees who might not have any physical documents to prove their identity. Additionally, the portability of digital IDs on blockchain allows refugees to carry their verified identities with them no matter where they go, without the need to carry physical documents that can be easily lost or stolen.

A notable application of blockchain for refugee digital identities is the ID2020 Alliance. This initiative harnesses the power of blockchain to provide refugees with digital identities. The ID2020 system allows for the recording of vital data such as birthdate, nationality, and biometrics, securely on the blockchain. These digital IDs empower refugees by enabling them to prove their identity and access critical services.

For instance, with a blockchain-based digital ID, refugees can access healthcare services without the typical bureaucratic hurdles that require government-issued identification. In education, these IDs can be used to enroll in schools and access learning opportunities, which are crucial for the integration and development of refugee children and adults into new societies. Furthermore, digital IDs allow refugees to open bank accounts and perform financial transactions, which are essential for managing remittances, receiving aid, and conducting day-to-day financial activities that are often taken for granted.

The ability to verify one's identity easily and securely also aids significantly in the social integration and mobility of refugees. Recognized digital IDs can smooth interactions with government agencies and non-governmental organizations, reducing the often-discriminatory obstacles that undocumented individuals face. Furthermore, these IDs facilitate legal processes, such as applying for asylum, securing work permits, or obtaining driver's licenses, which are essential steps towards stability and self-reliance in a new country.

While the ID2020 initiative and similar projects represent significant advances, challenges remain in their broader implementation. Issues such as global recognition of digital IDs, integration with existing governmental systems, and ensuring data privacy are critical areas that need addressing. Moreover, as these systems become more prevalent, ongoing efforts to maintain the security and integrity of the blockchain platforms are essential to protect against any potential cybersecurity threats. Blockchain technology's ability to provide secure, immutable, and portable digital identities offers a significant opportunity to improve the lives of refugees globally. By enabling access to essential services and aiding social integration, digital IDs hold the potential to transform the refugee experience, offering a pathway to greater stability and integration. As initiatives like ID2020 expand and evolve, they pave the way for a future where all individuals, regardless of their displacement status, can access the services and rights they need to thrive.

Despite its significant potential, blockchain technology is not without its challenges and limitations. Technological complexity and scalability issues are major concerns. Blockchain networks, especially those that operate on a large scale, often require substantial computational power, which can lead to inefficiencies and high costs. Additionally, the environmental impact of some blockchain implementations cannot be overlooked. Particularly, those that rely on energy-intensive consensus mechanisms like proof of work, which require extensive electricity use, posing significant environmental concerns.

The rapid development of blockchain technology necessitates the creation of comprehensive regulatory frameworks. These frameworks are crucial for guiding ethical innovation and ensuring that blockchain deployments protect users' rights and data while promoting transparency and accountability. The absence of such regulations can hinder the adoption and trust in blockchain technologies, as stakeholders may be wary of potential legal and ethical pitfalls.

Looking to the future, the integration of blockchain with other cutting-edge technologies such as artificial intelligence (AI) and the Internet of Things (IoT) presents promising opportunities. These technologies can complement blockchain by creating smarter, more responsive systems that enhance capabilities such as automated decision-making and real-time data analysis. For example, AI can be used to optimize blockchain operations, reducing energy consumption and improving transaction speeds, while IoT devices can securely transact and communicate valuable data across blockchain networks for applications ranging from smart homes to logistics.

When combined with purpose-driven leadership and strong ethical frameworks, blockchain technology has the capacity to drive substantial social and economic transformations. Purpose-driven leadership is particularly vital in steering the development and application of blockchain towards outcomes that are not only innovative but also equitable, sustainable, and inclusive. As blockchain technology continues to evolve, maintaining a focus on its application in social innovation is crucial. By doing so, it can effectively address some of the world's most pressing challenges, such as enhancing global supply chains, providing secure digital identities to the underserved, and ensuring transparency in governmental and corporate operations.

Ensuring the sustainable growth of blockchain technology will require ongoing efforts to balance innovation with ethical considerations, environmental sustainability, and regulatory compliance. By navigating these challenges thoughtfully, the future of blockchain could redefine a range of industries, offering solutions that are not just technologically advanced but also aligned with broader social goals.

Chapter 3: Leveraging Blockchain for Environmental Sustainability

In the pursuit of sustainable development, blockchain technology has rapidly emerged as a powerful tool, particularly in driving progressive environmental initiatives. Known for its unparalleled ability to enhance transparency and accountability, blockchain technology is ideally suited to tackle some of the most pressing environmental challenges facing our planet today. This section of the discussion explores the varied applications of blockchain designed to promote environmental sustainability. It underscores a series of successful initiatives where blockchain technology has not only facilitated substantial improvements in resource management and conservation efforts but also ensured that these efforts are conducted in a transparent and verifiable manner.

By offering detailed examples, we delve into how this innovative technology is being utilized across various sectors. One of the primary applications is in the tracking of renewable energy usage. Blockchain platforms enable the accurate and transparent recording of energy production and consumption, helping to optimize the balance between supply and demand in renewable energy markets. Another significant application is in managing carbon emissions. Through blockchain, companies can monitor and trade carbon credits more efficiently, ensuring that each credit is only used once and that all transactions are secure and transparent, thereby supporting global efforts to reduce carbon footprints.

Blockchain technology is revolutionizing the sustainability of supply chains. By providing a transparent ledger for supply chain transactions, blockchain allows for the precise tracking of products from their source to the consumer. This capability is crucial for verifying the sustainability of the materials used, ensuring ethical labor practices, and reducing waste and inefficiencies at various stages of the supply chain.

Through these examples, this exploration aims to highlight the transformative potential of blockchain in fostering a more sustainable and accountable approach to environmental stewardship. By integrating blockchain technology into environmental efforts, organizations are not only able to achieve greater operational efficiencies but are also empowered to make verifiable claims about their environmental impact, building trust with consumers, investors, and regulatory bodies. This alignment of technological innovation with eco-friendly practices presents a promising pathway toward achieving broader environmental goals and catalyzing global sustainable development.

One of the most promising applications of blockchain technology in promoting environmental sustainability is within the renewable energy sector. Blockchain platforms offer a unique capability to enhance the renewable energy market by enabling direct transactions between energy producers and consumers, effectively bypassing traditional energy markets and utility providers. This direct connection can lead to significant reductions in energy costs and increase the efficiency of energy distribution, particularly for renewable sources. A compelling example of this application is the Brooklyn Microgrid project in Brooklyn, New York. This innovative project utilizes blockchain technology to create a localized energy grid where residents can buy and sell solar power generated directly from their rooftops to their neighbors. This peer-to-peer energy trading model harnesses the power of blockchain to facilitate secure and transparent transactions without the need for traditional intermediaries.

The Brooklyn Microgrid not only supports the wider adoption of renewable energy by making it more accessible and economically viable but also enhances community resilience. By enabling a decentralized energy distribution model, communities can maintain power locally even when central grids face disruptions. This aspect of local resilience is particularly valuable in areas prone to extreme weather or other disruptions that might affect central power systems. The project serves as a powerful model for how blockchain can democratize energy production and consumption. Residents who produce surplus energy can sell it directly to their neighbors, fostering a sense of community while promoting sustainable energy practices. This setup incentivizes more residents to install solar panels and participate in the renewable energy economy, further expanding the environmental benefits.

The success of the Brooklyn Microgrid has significant implications for the future of energy management worldwide. It illustrates the potential for blockchain to transform the traditional energy sector, encouraging a shift towards more sustainable and resilient energy solutions. The project highlights how blockchain can be leveraged to not only improve the efficiency of transactions but also to empower communities, promote local energy independence, and support the global transition to renewable energy sources.

As blockchain technology continues to evolve, its potential to revolutionize the renewable energy sector grows, promising a future where communities can manage their energy needs in a more sustainable, efficient, and resilient manner. This development is particularly crucial as the world seeks to meet increasing energy demands while also addressing the urgent need for environmental sustainability.

Blockchain technology has the potential to significantly transform the carbon credit market, addressing longstanding issues of transparency and fraud. By utilizing blockchain to track and manage carbon credits securely, each credit is accounted for uniquely, ensuring that it can only be used once and preventing double-counting or fraudulent claims. This not only strengthens the reliability of carbon markets but also enhances their role in global efforts to combat climate change.
A leading example of this application is IBM's blockchain-based platform designed specifically for carbon trading. This innovative platform provides businesses with the tools to monitor and

manage their carbon emissions effectively. By integrating blockchain technology, the platform offers an immutable record of carbon credit transactions, which facilitates a transparent audit trail from the issuance of credits to their eventual retirement.

IBM's platform allows companies to track their carbon footprint in real-time, providing a clear view of their environmental impact. This visibility is crucial for companies committed to reducing their carbon emissions and for regulatory bodies looking to enforce environmental compliance. The blockchain ensures that all entries into the ledger are permanent and tamper-proof, making it easier for companies to prove compliance with environmental regulations and for auditors to verify carbon transactions without the possibility of manipulation. The increased efficiency and transparency provided by blockchain technology make carbon trading more accessible and appealing to a broader range of businesses. Smaller companies, which may have been deterred from participating in carbon markets due to the complexity and potential for fraud, can now engage more confidently. This broader participation can enhance the liquidity of the carbon market, making it a more effective tool for financing emission reduction projects across various sectors.

The use of blockchain in carbon credit markets also aligns with broader environmental goals by ensuring that the process of trading carbon credits genuinely contributes to the reduction of global carbon emissions. By providing a trustworthy and efficient system for carbon trading, blockchain can help ensure that environmental goals are met and that the impact of each credit towards mitigating climate change is clearly documented and understood.

IBM's initiative exemplifies how blockchain technology can be leveraged to foster a fairer, more transparent, and more efficient carbon trading market. This advancement is particularly significant as the world increasingly turns to market-based mechanisms to address environmental challenges. As blockchain technology continues to evolve, its application in environmental finance like carbon trading will likely play a crucial role in global sustainability efforts, promoting a cleaner, more accountable, and more sustainable future.

Blockchain technology plays a pivotal role in promoting sustainable supply chains by enhancing transparency and accountability from the source to the consumer. In modern supply chains, it is often challenging for companies and consumers to verify the origins and processing of products, particularly when it comes to ensuring that they are ethically sourced and sustainably managed. Blockchain's inherent characteristics of immutability and transparency make it an ideal tool for tracking the lifecycle of products and verifying the sustainability practices of suppliers along the way.

A significant application of blockchain in promoting sustainable supply chains can be seen in the tracking of tuna in the Pacific. This initiative utilizes blockchain technology to monitor tuna from the moment it is caught until it reaches the store shelf. The project involves recording each step of the tuna's journey on a blockchain ledger, from capture and processing to its final sale. This detailed tracking system ensures that the tuna has been fished using sustainable methods and that all fishing regulations have been adhered to, providing a clear, tamper-proof record.

The transparency provided by blockchain allows consumers to access the complete history of the product by scanning a QR code or accessing a database linked to the blockchain. This transparency not only empowers consumers to make informed purchasing decisions based on sustainability practices but also pressures companies to adhere to ethical standards. By enabling consumers to see whether the tuna has been legally caught and if sustainable fishing practices have been employed, blockchain helps combat illegal fishing activities that contribute to overfishing and ecological destruction. This initiative also benefits regulators and environmental groups by providing them with a reliable and accurate tool to enforce fishing laws and to monitor the impact of fishing on marine ecosystems. The ability to trace the exact route and handling of each batch of tuna makes it significantly easier to identify discrepancies or illegal activities along the supply chain.

In addition to promoting sustainability in the fishing industry, blockchain technology can be applied to various other sectors requiring detailed tracking and verification of supply chain practices. For example, in agriculture, blockchain can be used to ensure that crops are grown without harmful pesticides or that labor practices meet ethical standards. In manufacturing, it can verify that materials are sourced sustainably and that products are made in compliance with environmental regulations.

The use of blockchain in supply chains represents a powerful approach to ensuring that products are sourced and produced responsibly. This technology not only supports the enforcement of regulatory compliance but also enhances consumer trust and corporate accountability, ultimately leading to more sustainable business practices and better conservation of global resources. As more industries adopt blockchain to manage their supply chains, the potential for widespread positive impact on sustainability grows exponentially.

Blockchain technology is increasingly recognized as a transformative tool for enhancing waste management and recycling processes. By enabling transparent tracking of waste streams, blockchain can significantly improve the oversight and management of waste from its generation to final recycling or disposal. This enhanced traceability ensures that waste is handled properly according to environmental regulations and standards.

A particularly innovative application of blockchain in this domain is the use of tokenization systems to incentivize recycling behaviors. These systems can transform the act of recycling from a mere environmental responsibility into a rewarding activity that offers tangible benefits. An exemplary initiative in this area is undertaken by Plastic Bank, an organization that leverages blockchain technology to tackle plastic pollution effectively. Plastic Bank has developed a system where individuals who collect plastic waste can exchange it for digital tokens secured by blockchain. This approach not only provides a secure and transparent way to track the quantities of plastic collected and recycled but also monetizes the waste, turning it into a form of currency.

The process works by assigning a value to the plastic waste, which can then be traded for goods, services, or even cash. This system incentivizes community members, particularly in regions heavily impacted by plastic pollution, to engage in collection efforts. By providing economic incentives, it motivates broader participation in recycling activities, thereby increasing the amount of plastic that is diverted from landfills and oceans. The transparency afforded by blockchain ensures that the data regarding the amount of plastic collected and recycled is accurate and tamper-proof. This transparency is crucial for gaining the trust of participants and stakeholders, including donors and partners who support the recycling initiatives. It also allows for the effective tracking of the environmental impact of the recycling efforts, providing clear evidence of the reduction in plastic pollution.

This model not only helps mitigate environmental damage but also fosters a circular economy where plastic waste is viewed as a valuable resource rather than mere trash. It empowers impoverished communities by providing them with an opportunity to earn a stable income through environmental conservation activities, thus addressing both socio-economic and environmental issues simultaneously.

As blockchain technology continues to evolve, its potential to revolutionize waste management and recycling becomes more apparent. Projects like Plastic Bank are just the beginning, illustrating how blockchain can be utilized to enhance sustainability efforts worldwide. This approach not only improves environmental outcomes but also supports sustainable development goals, paving the way for more innovative uses of blockchain in managing waste and promoting recycling on a global scale.

Accurate environmental data is essential for effective environmental management and policymaking. Blockchain technology offers a robust solution by enhancing the reliability, transparency, and accessibility of this data. Through blockchain, data collected from various environmental monitoring activities can be secured against tampering, ensuring its integrity while making it readily accessible for analysis and decision-making.

An excellent example of blockchain's application in environmental monitoring is seen in the use of a network of air quality sensors across a city. These sensors are connected via a blockchain network, which collects and records data on pollution levels in real-time. The integration of blockchain ensures that once data is recorded, it cannot be altered or falsified, maintaining the accuracy and reliability of the information.

This system allows for continuous monitoring of air quality, providing a clear and accurate assessment of pollution levels at any given time. The data collected is not only secure but also made publicly accessible on the blockchain. This transparency is crucial as it allows citizens to be informed about the air quality in their environment, fostering greater public awareness and participation in pollution control efforts.

For policymakers, the reliable and real-time data provided by the blockchain-enabled sensor network is invaluable. It enables more informed decision-making, allowing for the implementation of timely and effective environmental protection measures. Policies can be adapted dynamically based on accurate, up-to-the-minute data, enhancing the responsiveness of actions to mitigate pollution. The availability of this data can spur community initiatives and empower local actions aimed at reducing pollution. Community groups, non-governmental organizations, and educational institutions can use the data to advocate for changes, educate the public, and monitor the effectiveness of local policies.

In addition to enhancing air quality monitoring, blockchain's application in environmental data management can be expanded to other areas such as water quality assessment, wildlife tracking, and monitoring deforestation activities. In each case, blockchain can provide a secure, transparent, and decentralized platform for collecting, storing, and sharing critical environmental data.

The use of blockchain for monitoring and reporting environmental data not only increases the accuracy and reliability of this information but also promotes a more inclusive and responsive approach to environmental protection. By ensuring data integrity and public access, blockchain empowers both policymakers and the general public to take more effective actions toward a sustainable and healthy environment. Innovation in blockchain technology is critical for enhancing its role in environmental sustainability. Innovations that improve blockchain's energy efficiency, scalability, and accessibility can broaden its impact and enable more widespread adoption. For instance, the development of more energy-efficient consensus algorithms, like proof-of-stake (PoS), addresses concerns over the high energy consumption associated with traditional proof-of-work (PoW) systems used in networks like Bitcoin. By reducing the energy demand, these innovations make blockchain more environmentally friendly and sustainable for widespread use.

The integration of blockchain with other technologies such as the Internet of Things (IoT) and big data analytics significantly enhances its capability to drive environmental sustainability. IoT devices can collect vast amounts of environmental data, such as temperature, pollution levels, or energy usage, which can be securely stored and managed on a blockchain. This integration enables more accurate monitoring and reporting of environmental conditions, leading to better-informed decision-making in environmental management and policy.

Consider a smart cities initiative where blockchain is integrated with IoT devices across the city to optimize energy use and reduce emissions. Smart sensors could monitor energy consumption in real-time, with data recorded on a blockchain to ensure transparency and immutability. This system could automatically adjust energy use in public buildings based on real-time data, significantly reducing waste and promoting energy efficiency.

Blockchain technology fosters collaboration between different stakeholders in the environmental sector by providing a trustworthy platform for data sharing and communication. This can be particularly impactful in large-scale environmental projects that require coordination across various geographical and administrative boundaries. By using blockchain to manage and verify data from multiple sources, stakeholders can work together more effectively, aligning their efforts towards common environmental goals.

In global reforestation projects, blockchain can be used to verify and track the origin, species, and maintenance of planted trees across different countries. This ensures that contributions to reforestation efforts are accurately recorded and maintained, encouraging more organizations and individuals to participate in these initiatives knowing their efforts are transparently managed and contribute to verifiable environmental benefits.

Blockchain can significantly aid in regulatory compliance and reporting by automating these processes and making them more transparent. Smart contracts can be programmed to execute automatically when certain regulatory conditions are met, such as emissions reporting or adherence to waste management protocols. This not only streamlines the compliance process but also reduces the possibility of human error or fraud. An environmental compliance platform powered by blockchain could automatically collect data from industrial entities, verify it against regulatory requirements, and report compliance status to relevant authorities. Such a platform would ensure that all data is accurate and tamper-proof, enhancing trust between regulators, businesses, and the public.

Blockchain also plays a role in influencing consumer behavior towards more sustainable practices. By providing transparency about the environmental impact of products or services, blockchain can empower consumers to make informed decisions based on sustainability criteria. This demand for transparency can drive companies to adopt more sustainable practices to meet consumer expectations.

A mobile app utilizing blockchain could provide consumers with detailed information about the environmental impact of products at the point of sale, such as the carbon footprint of manufacturing, packaging, and transport. Such transparent insight could motivate consumers to choose products that are more environmentally friendly, driving companies to focus more on sustainability in their production processes.

Innovation is pivotal in enhancing the role of blockchain in promoting environmental sustainability. By continuing to develop and integrate new technologies, improving energy efficiency, and fostering collaboration, blockchain can significantly contribute to the global effort to combat environmental challenges. As more stakeholders recognize and invest in these innovative solutions, blockchain's potential to support a sustainable future becomes increasingly tangible and impactful. In this chapter, we examined the significant impact of blockchain technology on enhancing environmental sustainability. The discussion illuminated how blockchain can revolutionize transparency, accountability, and resource management across various sectors, contributing positively to environmental stewardship.

This chapter began with an exploration of blockchain's application in renewable energy markets, exemplified by the Brooklyn Microgrid project. This initiative enables decentralized, peer-to-peer energy transactions, empowering communities to manage their energy consumption sustainably and support resilient energy infrastructures. We also explored the transformative potential of blockchain in carbon credit markets, highlighting IBM's blockchain-based platform as a case study. This platform significantly enhances the transparency and efficiency of carbon trading, ensuring that environmental objectives are achieved through reliable and transparent trading mechanisms. The narrative then shifted to sustainable supply chains, where blockchain's ability to ensure transparency and traceability was demonstrated through the tuna tracking initiative in the Pacific. This use case illustrated blockchain's effectiveness in verifying sustainable practices and combating illegal fishing, thereby promoting ethical sourcing and management. The discussion also covered blockchain's role in waste management and recycling, as illustrated by the Plastic Bank initiative. This project creatively employs blockchain for tokenization to incentivize recycling, showcasing a novel approach to reducing plastic pollution and enhancing environmental sustainability.

Chapter 4: Advancing Social Equity with Blockchain Technology

Blockchain technology is increasingly recognized not only as a disruptor of economic systems but also as a powerful tool for advancing social equity. This technology's inherent capabilities can significantly contribute to leveling societal playing fields by enhancing transparency and broadening access in several key areas. This chapter delves into how blockchain can be utilized to promote greater transparency in supply chains and improve financial inclusion—two domains where technology can substantially influence equality and access.

One of the critical applications of blockchain in promoting social equity is in supply chain management. By providing an immutable and transparent record of every transaction or product movement, blockchain technology helps ensure that all stakeholders in the supply chain—from producers to end consumers—have access to the same information, thereby reducing the chances of fraud and exploitation. This transparency is particularly crucial in industries like agriculture and manufacturing, where it can help ensure fair wages and safe working conditions for workers. Furthermore, consumers increasingly demand ethically sourced products, and blockchain enables companies to prove the provenance of their goods, ensuring that they meet social and environmental standards.

Blockchain also holds significant promise for enhancing financial inclusion, a fundamental aspect of social equity. Many people around the world remain unbanked or underbanked and lack access to traditional financial services. Blockchain technology can bridge this gap by providing these individuals with access to financial products and services, such as secure savings accounts, loans, and insurance, without the need for a traditional bank account. For example, through decentralized finance (DeFi) platforms, individuals can engage in financial transactions and access services that are typically reserved for those with conventional banking relationships. This not only includes the ability to transact but also the opportunity to build credit and improve their financial stability.

The chapter will explore various case studies and initiatives where blockchain technology has been successfully implemented to enhance social equity. These examples will illustrate the practical applications of blockchain in both supply chain transparency and financial inclusion, providing insights into how technology has been used to solve real-world problems in these areas. By examining successful models, this section aims to showcase the potential scalability of such solutions and encourage more widespread adoption of blockchain technology in efforts to promote social equity.

This chapter of the book aims to highlight how blockchain technology can be a critical ally in the quest for social equity. By leveraging blockchain's capabilities to enhance transparency in supply chains and improve financial inclusion, it is possible to address some of the fundamental disparities that persist in modern society, paving the way for a more equitable world. Transparency in supply chains is a critical component in ensuring that ethical practices are upheld across various industries. From improving labor conditions to minimizing environmental impact, transparency helps ensure that operations meet ethical and regulatory standards. Blockchain technology plays a pivotal role in achieving this transparency by providing an immutable and transparent record-keeping system that traces products from their origin to the end consumer.

Blockchain's ability to offer a verifiable and tamper-proof digital ledger means that every transaction along the supply chain can be recorded and traced. This capability allows for the detailed tracking of a product's journey—from raw materials extraction through manufacturing processes to final delivery. By doing so, blockchain enables all parties involved, including suppliers, manufacturers, distributors, and consumers, to access the same information regarding the origins and handling of the products. For instance, in industries such as agriculture or apparel, where sourcing and labor practices often come under scrutiny, blockchain can provide reassurance that goods have not been produced under exploitative conditions. Consumers increasingly demand ethical production, and blockchain provides a way for companies to prove their compliance with labor laws and ethical standards. This can enhance brand trust and loyalty among consumers who prioritize sustainability and social responsibility.

Blockchain facilitates greater accountability. If every step of a product's production and distribution is recorded, companies are more likely to adhere to environmental standards and labor laws, knowing that any deviation is detectable and traceable. Regulatory bodies can also use blockchain records to enforce compliance more effectively, as the technology provides a reliable audit trail. In addition to tracking physical goods, blockchain can be used to monitor and verify other aspects of the supply chain, such as carbon footprints and energy use. Companies can use blockchain to record and publicly report on their environmental impact measures, which supports transparency and helps them to meet regulatory requirements and consumer expectations for sustainable practices.

The implementation of blockchain for transparent supply chains not only aids in enforcing ethical standards but also enhances efficiency. By reducing discrepancies and errors in record-keeping, blockchain can streamline operations, reduce delays, and cut costs related to documentation and verification processes.

Blockchain technology is transforming supply chain management by embedding transparency and integrity into global supply networks. This shift not only helps protect the rights of workers and reduce environmental damage but also strengthens consumer confidence and improves the overall sustainability of business operations. As more industries adopt blockchain for supply chain transparency, we can expect to see significant advancements in the way companies manage their ethical responsibilities and regulatory obligations.

The coffee industry, known for its complex supply chains, is a prime candidate for the implementation of blockchain technology to enhance transparency and ensure ethical practices. In this industry, coffee beans typically pass through numerous hands—from farmers to intermediaries, exporters, roasters, and finally, retailers—before reaching consumers. This lengthy chain can often obscure critical information about the origin of the coffee and the conditions under which it was produced. By integrating blockchain technology, each step of the coffee's journey can be recorded in a secure, immutable ledger. This includes detailed information about where the coffee was grown, the methods used in its cultivation, how it was harvested, the wages paid to workers, and the conditions under which they worked. For example, as soon as coffee beans are harvested and bagged, a digital record is created on the blockchain. This record can include data such as the date and location of harvest, the identity of the farmer, and the price paid for the beans. As the beans move through the supply chain—from local cooperatives to global shippers to roasters—the blockchain is updated with new transactions, each linked securely to the previous one, creating a comprehensive and tamper-proof chain of custody.

This level of traceability and transparency is transformative. For consumers, it means having access to verifiable data about the coffee they purchase. This not only enables them to make informed choices based on their values but also enhances their trust in brands that prove their commitment to fairness and quality. Consumers can scan a QR code on a package of coffee to access a detailed history of its journey, empowering them with knowledge about the product's ethical credentials.

For businesses, the pressure to uphold ethical standards is significantly increased. The transparency ensured by blockchain means that any unethical practices in the supply chain can be more easily detected by consumers, regulators, and certification bodies such as Fair Trade. This visibility encourages businesses to adhere strictly to ethical guidelines, knowing that their practices are open to scrutiny. Blockchain technology can facilitate fairer transactions within the coffee supply chain. By automating payments through smart contracts, for instance, farmers can be assured of receiving timely and fair compensation for their products, directly linked to the fulfillment of contract terms. This can help address the economic disparities often seen in traditional coffee supply chains, where farmers receive only a small fraction of the final retail price.

The use of blockchain in the coffee industry represents a significant step toward more ethical, transparent, and fair-trade practices. It not only supports the rights and livelihoods of farmers but also meets the growing consumer demand for responsibly sourced products. As blockchain technology continues to evolve and expand, its potential to revolutionize traditional supply chains and promote global fairness and sustainability becomes increasingly clear.

Enhancing financial inclusion through blockchain technology represents a transformative opportunity to address the significant disparities in access to financial services worldwide. Currently, a substantial portion of the global population remains unbanked or underbanked, lacking access to essential financial services such as savings accounts, credit, or insurance. This exclusion from the traditional financial system severely limits their economic opportunities and ability to secure financial stability. Blockchain technology, with its decentralized nature, offers a radical solution to this challenge, potentially democratizing access to financial services across the globe.

Blockchain technology enables the creation of decentralized financial services (DeFi) that do not rely on traditional banking infrastructures. Instead, these services utilize blockchain's secure, peer-to-peer architecture to provide a wide range of financial transactions that are accessible to anyone with a smartphone and an internet connection. This accessibility is particularly transformative in rural or underserved areas where traditional banking infrastructure is limited or non-existent.

Through blockchain platforms, individuals can engage in micro-lending activities, receive and send remittances at lower costs, participate in crowdfunding initiatives, and access digital wallets where they can securely store and manage their funds. These services are typically facilitated by user-friendly applications that do not require users to have a formal bank account, thus lowering the barrier to entry for many people who have been excluded from the financial system.

Blockchain's inherent features of transparency and security play a crucial role in building trust among users. Every transaction recorded on a blockchain is immutable and transparent, which means that it cannot be altered once it has been executed and can be viewed by all parties involved. This level of transparency ensures that users can see exactly where their money is going and how it is being used, which builds confidence in the financial services provided. The implementation of smart contracts on blockchain platforms automates the execution of agreements without the need for intermediaries. This automation reduces the transaction costs and speeds up the processing time, making financial services more efficient and affordable for users. For example, smart contracts can automatically execute payments upon the fulfillment of specific conditions, such as the repayment of a loan, which simplifies and secures the transaction process.

The impact of blockchain on financial inclusion extends beyond individual transactions; it has the potential to integrate the unbanked into the global economy. By providing the unbanked with tools to save, invest, and grow their resources, blockchain technology can help bridge the economic divide and empower individuals with greater control over their financial future.

Blockchain-based microfinance and peer-to-peer lending platforms represent a significant breakthrough in extending financial services to the unbanked, fundamentally transforming how these individuals can access capital. Traditionally, securing loans without a bank account or a formal credit history has been a significant hurdle for millions in developing regions, effectively barring them from entering the formal economy or expanding small businesses. However, blockchain technology offers a viable solution by enabling secure, transparent, and accessible financial transactions.

These platforms operate on the principle of decentralization, eliminating the need for traditional financial intermediaries such as banks. Instead, they connect borrowers directly with lenders through a secure, digital ledger that records all transactions. This direct connection not only reduces the costs associated with loans—by cutting out middlemen—but also speeds up the process, making funds available more quickly to those in need.

The security and transparency provided by blockchain are crucial in reducing the risks associated with lending to underserved populations. Each transaction on a blockchain-based platform is recorded in a way that is immutable and transparent, ensuring that all parties can track the movement of funds and the terms of the loan agreement. This visibility helps build trust among users, who can be confident that their transactions are secure and that the terms of their agreements will be honored.

Blockchain's transparency plays a pivotal role in attracting more lenders to these platforms. Investors seeking to fund micro-enterprises and startups in developing regions often hesitate due to the perceived risk and lack of reliable information. Blockchain platforms can mitigate these concerns by providing a clear record of borrowers' repayment histories and the use of funds, thereby encouraging more investments. By demonstrating a reliable track of financial behavior, borrowers can build their creditworthiness over time within the blockchain ecosystem, further facilitating their access to larger loans. These platforms can implement innovative approaches to credit assessment, which do not rely solely on traditional credit scores. Instead, they can use alternative data—such as transaction history, mobile phone usage, or even social network data—to assess a borrower's creditworthiness. This method opens up opportunities for individuals who have been financially invisible to access capital based on their actual financial behavior and trustworthiness.

Blockchain-based microfinance and peer-to-peer lending platforms not only provide essential financial services to the unbanked but also empower them to take control of their economic futures. They allow individuals to secure loans for personal use, grow micro-enterprises, or fund startups, contributing significantly to economic development in their communities. As these platforms continue to evolve and expand, they hold the promise of fostering a more inclusive financial landscape globally, where access to capital is based on trust and transparency, not just credit history or banking access.

The implementation of blockchain technology across various sectors, particularly in enhancing supply chain transparency and promoting financial inclusion, is poised to have transformative impacts on societal structures. These changes not only affect economic dynamics but also encourage shifts in social behavior and corporate responsibility. By improving transparency in supply chains, blockchain technology drives a major shift towards more responsible consumer behavior and corporate practices. When consumers have access to detailed information about the origins and journey of the products they purchase, they can make more informed choices that align with their values concerning environmental sustainability and social responsibility. This heightened consumer awareness and demand for transparency compel companies to adopt more responsible practices. As a result, businesses are incentivized to improve their supply chains, ensuring that their products are ethically sourced and that all stakeholders in the supply chain, from farmers to factory workers, are treated fairly and sustainably. This can lead to improvements in working conditions and pay, as well as encourage companies to adopt environmentally friendly practices to meet consumer expectations.

Blockchain's impact on financial inclusion introduces significant opportunities for economic empowerment among marginalized communities. By providing access to financial services via blockchain platforms, individuals in underbanked regions can participate in economic activities that were previously beyond their reach. For example, through blockchain-based financial services, small business owners in remote areas can receive microloans to expand their businesses, families can securely save money for future needs, and entrepreneurs can access global markets. This access to financial tools enables individuals and communities to build wealth and stability, reducing poverty and fostering overall economic growth.

These economic opportunities can have far-reaching effects on societal structures. They promote greater economic equity, reduce disparities, and catalyze upward social mobility for individuals and communities that were previously marginalized. Moreover, as more people gain access to financial services, there is a broader distribution of economic power, which can lead to more resilient local economies and less dependence on external financial aid.

The systemic changes driven by blockchain in these areas are profound. In supply chains, the move towards transparency and ethical practices can lead to industry-wide shifts where sustainability becomes a core component of business operations rather than an optional add-on. In finance, the disruption brought by blockchain creates a more inclusive financial system that not only challenges but potentially replaces traditional banking structures with more democratized financial services. The implementation of blockchain technology fosters a transition towards a more equitable and responsible world. The shift towards transparent supply chains and inclusive financial services not only empowers individuals and transforms communities but also redefines the role of businesses in society. As blockchain continues to break down barriers and democratize access to information and resources, its potential to reshape societal structures globally continues to unfold.

While the potential of blockchain to enhance social equity is indeed vast, the journey towards fully realizing this potential involves overcoming several significant barriers. These challenges range from technological access issues to regulatory and scalability concerns, each requiring strategic solutions to ensure that blockchain can deliver on its promises of social equity.

One of the foremost challenges is the digital divide that prevents widespread access to blockchain technologies. This divide is particularly pronounced in underdeveloped or rural areas where access to reliable internet and modern digital devices is limited. Without the necessary technological infrastructure, the benefits of blockchain, such as improved financial inclusion and transparent supply chains, remain out of reach for many. Bridging this divide requires investment in infrastructure to bring internet connectivity and blockchain-enabled services to underserved areas. Additionally, it involves educating communities about blockchain technology and how to utilize it, which necessitates tailored educational programs that can address diverse levels of literacy and tech-savviness.

Another significant barrier is the need for comprehensive regulatory frameworks that protect users while fostering innovation. Blockchain operates in a complex legal landscape since it often transcends traditional geographic and jurisdictional boundaries. Developing regulations that can adapt to the decentralized and international nature of blockchain is essential. These regulations must ensure consumer protection, data privacy, and security without stifling the innovative potential of blockchain technologies. This requires a delicate balance, where policymakers work closely with technology experts and stakeholders to create informed, flexible regulatory frameworks that can adapt as the technology and its applications evolve.

Scaling blockchain solutions to have a meaningful global impact presents a substantial challenge. While pilot projects and small-scale implementations have shown promise, expanding these solutions to operate on a global scale involves complex logistics and significant resources. Issues such as interoperability between different blockchain systems, the environmental impact of large-scale blockchain operations, and the integration of these technologies into existing systems all need to be addressed. For blockchain to truly enhance social equity globally, solutions must not only be technically scalable but also economically viable and environmentally sustainable.

Overcoming these barriers requires cultivating an ecosystem that supports the widespread adoption of blockchain for social equity. This involves not only technological and regulatory advancements but also the creation of partnerships among governments, non-profits, technology providers, and the private sector. These collaborations are crucial in pooling resources, sharing knowledge, and aligning efforts towards common goals of enhancing transparency, accessibility, and inclusivity through blockchain. While the barriers to blockchain adoption for enhancing social equity are significant, they are not insurmountable. With strategic investments in technology access, thoughtful regulatory approaches, and efforts to scale solutions responsibly, blockchain technology holds the promise of being a powerful tool for promoting fairness and equity across global societies. Blockchain technology is increasingly recognized for its transformative potential in the field of humanitarian aid. By leveraging its intrinsic characteristics of transparency and immutability, blockchain provides a reliable mechanism for tracking and distributing aid, ensuring that resources are delivered effectively and equitably to those in need. This capability is particularly critical in humanitarian contexts, where the misappropriation of resources and corruption can significantly hinder relief efforts.

In humanitarian aid scenarios, blockchain can be employed to manage and distribute donations of money, goods, and services transparently. Every transaction recorded on a blockchain ledger is traceable and irreversible, which significantly reduces the risk of fraud and mismanagement. This system allows donors to see exactly how their contributions are being used, enhancing donor confidence and potentially increasing the willingness of individuals and organizations to contribute to aid initiatives.

The use of blockchain in humanitarian aid extends beyond financial transactions to include the distribution of resources like food, medical supplies, and housing. By tagging these resources with digital tokens on a blockchain, organizations can track their distribution from origin to final delivery, ensuring that aid reaches the intended recipients. This method also helps to prevent the duplication of aid delivery, a common issue in disaster-stricken areas where communication between multiple aid organizations may be fragmented.

Blockchain also facilitates greater coordination among different stakeholders involved in humanitarian efforts, including NGOs, government agencies, and international organizations. By providing a single, shared platform for recording and accessing data, blockchain can help synchronize efforts and ensure that aid is distributed in a more organized and efficient manner. This coordination is crucial in emergency situations, where timely and organized aid delivery can save lives. Blockchain platforms can empower recipients by giving them control over their aid through digital wallets and identity verification systems. This approach not only respects the dignity of aid recipients by involving them directly in the aid process but also allows them to access and utilize aid according to their specific needs.

An example of blockchain's application in humanitarian aid is its use to facilitate the distribution of financial assistance to refugees. By using blockchain-based digital wallets, refugees can receive and spend their aid funds securely without the need for a traditional bank account. This system not only provides refugees with immediate access to funds but also integrates them into the financial system, providing a foundation for longer-term financial stability.

Blockchain's application in humanitarian aid exemplifies its capacity to enhance social equity by improving the transparency, efficiency, and integrity of aid distribution. As this technology continues to evolve, its role in reshaping humanitarian efforts offers a promising avenue for addressing some of the most pressing challenges faced by vulnerable populations around the world. The UN World Food Programme (WFP) has pioneered an innovative application of blockchain technology through its Building Blocks project, designed to enhance the distribution and management of aid in refugee camps. This project harnesses the power of blockchain to ensure that aid distribution is both secure and transparent, directly addressing the challenges of misallocation and inefficiency that often plague humanitarian efforts.

One of the significant achievements of the Building Blocks project has been its ability to reduce transaction costs associated with distributing aid. Traditionally, humanitarian aid distribution involves multiple intermediaries, each adding layers of complexity and cost. Blockchain technology enables the WFP to bypass these intermediaries, directly connecting aid providers with beneficiaries. This direct connection is made possible by blockchain's decentralized nature, which allows for secure, transparent transactions without the need for a central verifying authority. As a result, the project has dramatically reduced costs associated with fees and has minimized the potential for funds to be siphoned off by middlemen.

Another critical advantage of the Building Blocks project is its ability to ensure that aid reaches its intended recipients. Each transaction within the system is recorded on a secure, immutable ledger, providing a clear, auditable trail from donor to beneficiary. This traceability is crucial in contexts where corruption and theft can divert essential resources away from those in dire need. Beneficiaries receive aid through digital tokens or vouchers, which they can use to purchase food and supplies securely within the camp. This method not only ensures that aid is spent as intended but also empowers recipients by giving them the autonomy to choose what they need most.

The transparent nature of blockchain also enhances accountability in aid distribution. Donors and stakeholders can track the flow of resources and verify that aid is being used appropriately. This transparency helps build trust among donors and supports increased funding for humanitarian efforts. Furthermore, it holds all parties involved in the distribution process accountable, from aid organizations to local suppliers, fostering a more ethical and responsible approach to aid delivery.

The Building Blocks project empowers beneficiaries by providing them with a secure digital identity. For many refugees and displaced individuals, a lack of official identification is a significant barrier to accessing services and exercising rights. The blockchain-based system used by the WFP allows for the creation of digital identities that are secure and portable, enabling refugees to receive aid and access services without traditional forms of ID.

The success of the Building Blocks project in pilot implementations has set the stage for its expansion to other regions and contexts. Its ability to improve the efficiency and integrity of aid distribution suggests a broad potential for blockchain technology in various aspects of humanitarian aid and development work. As the project scales, it could serve as a model for other organizations seeking to improve the effectiveness of aid delivery through technology.

The UN World Food Programme's Building Blocks project illustrates the profound impact blockchain technology can have on improving the delivery and management of humanitarian aid. By reducing costs, ensuring aid reaches those who need it most, enhancing transparency, and empowering beneficiaries, blockchain is proving to be an invaluable tool in the global effort to improve humanitarian responses. Blockchain technology presents a unique opportunity to advance social equity by promoting transparency in supply chains and extending financial services to the unbanked. As stakeholders continue to explore these applications, it is crucial to address existing barriers and ensure that blockchain initiatives are inclusive, equitable, and scalable. With the right approach, blockchain can significantly contribute to building a more equitable society, where transparency, access, and fairness are not just ideals but realities.

Blockchain companies can promote inclusivity and diversity through various effective strategies. First, they can establish a clear vision and values statement that emphasizes a commitment to inclusion and the value of diverse perspectives. This approach not only sets a foundational tone but also aligns the organization's actions with its broader goals.

These companies can actively engage with diverse communities, including customers, users, partners, and other stakeholders. By gathering their insights, feedback, and concerns and involving them in decision-making, blockchain solutions can be tailored to cater to a broad spectrum of needs. Providing education and empowerment opportunities is another critical strategy. Accessible resources, training programs, hackathons, incubators, and other initiatives help democratize access to blockchain opportunities and encourage wider participation.

Regular assessment of diversity and inclusion metrics and gathering feedback from stakeholders are essential. Making improvements based on these insights allows companies to track progress and address any emerging issues or gaps. Offering cross-training and interdisciplinary learning opportunities for both technologists and business leaders can foster a more inclusive culture and diverse skill sets within the organization. Adopting a proactive and intentional approach to creating a culture of belonging, valuing diverse perspectives, and empowering broad participation is crucial for fostering inclusivity in the blockchain industry.

Chapter 5: Governance Issues, Ethical Leadership Challenges in Cryptocurrency

As blockchain technology matures, it increasingly encounters complex ethical and regulatory landscapes that must be navigated with precision and foresight. Purpose-driven leaders are vital in steering these innovations towards positive societal impacts while maintaining compliance with evolving regulatory standards. These leaders play a pivotal role in advocating for fair regulations that enhance transparency, protect consumers, and encourage healthy market competition, all while fostering innovation.

Ethical leadership in blockchain is not just about compliance; it's about setting a standard for integrity and accountability in technology deployment. This involves making hard decisions that balance innovation with societal welfare, emphasizing the importance of ethical considerations in every phase of blockchain application.

Despite the clear benefits, blockchain and cryptocurrency technologies often encounter substantial trust barriers that hinder broader adoption. These barriers primarily arise from the inherent complexity of the technology, a general lack of understanding among the public, and past associations with illegal activities, such as money laundering and black-market transactions. Addressing these challenges is crucial for the wider acceptance and realization of blockchain's potential in facilitating social innovation.

Purpose-driven leadership plays a pivotal role in overcoming these trust barriers. Leaders in the blockchain community need to actively demonstrate the positive impacts of blockchain on society and the environment. This involves not just developing but also prioritizing and publicizing projects that yield tangible benefits. For example, initiatives that enhance financial inclusion can provide underserved communities with access to banking services, thus demonstrating the social value of blockchain. Similarly, projects that leverage blockchain for tracking carbon emissions or improving supply chain transparency directly showcase the technology's ability to reduce environmental impacts and enhance corporate accountability.

By focusing on such projects, leaders can help reshape public perception of blockchain and cryptocurrencies. This is vital because public attitudes often stem from a lack of understanding of how blockchain works and what it can achieve beyond the realm of digital currencies. Educational campaigns and transparent communication about the workings, benefits, and successful outcomes of blockchain initiatives play a critical role in demystifying the technology for the wider public. By illustrating the real-world applications and benefits of blockchain, leaders can foster a broader acceptance and trust in the technology. This involves not only highlighting successful projects but also addressing and mitigating the legitimate concerns people may have about privacy, security, and the ethical use of blockchain technology. The role of purpose-driven leaders is not only to advocate for the adoption of blockchain technology but also to ensure that its implementation is aligned with ethical standards and contributes positively to societal goals. Through strategic leadership, transparent practices, and a commitment to demonstrating tangible benefits, the trust in and adoption of blockchain technology can significantly increase, allowing it to fully realize its potential as a tool for social and environmental good.

The decentralized nature of blockchain and the anonymity provided by cryptocurrencies can create significant ethical challenges. These technologies offer groundbreaking opportunities for innovation, yet they also open doors to potential misuse if not guided by strong ethical principles. Purpose-driven leaders play a crucial role in navigating these challenges, ensuring that blockchain and cryptocurrencies are used to benefit society as a whole.

One of the primary responsibilities of these leaders is to develop and enforce frameworks and standards that address the unique ethical concerns associated with blockchain technology. This includes implementing measures that prevent misuse such as fraud, money laundering, or other illegal activities that could exploit the anonymity and lack of central oversight inherent in blockchain networks. Additionally, these frameworks must focus on protecting user privacy and ensuring robust data security to maintain trust and integrity within blockchain systems.

Guiding ethical innovation in blockchain extends beyond preventing misuse. Leaders must also consider the broader societal and environmental implications of deploying blockchain technology. For example, the significant energy consumption required by some blockchain operations, particularly those that use proof-of-work consensus mechanisms, poses serious environmental concerns. Ethical leadership in this context involves advocating for or developing more energy-efficient technologies that mitigate the environmental impact of blockchain operations.

As blockchain technology has the potential to disrupt traditional industries, ethical leaders must carefully consider the societal impacts of this disruption. For instance, the introduction of smart contracts and decentralized finance (DeFi) platforms can transform the financial industry, potentially displacing jobs and altering economic structures. Ethical leadership involves ensuring that such transitions do not exacerbate inequality or social division but rather are managed in ways that contribute to overall societal benefit.

Leaders must also ensure that the benefits of blockchain innovations are distributed equitably. This involves promoting inclusivity in access to blockchain technologies, ensuring that underserved and marginalized communities can also benefit from the innovations brought about by blockchain and cryptocurrencies. By fostering inclusivity, leaders can help prevent a digital divide that could otherwise widen socio-economic disparities.

Guiding ethical innovation in the realm of blockchain and cryptocurrencies is a multifaceted endeavor that requires purpose-driven leaders to navigate complex ethical landscapes. By developing robust frameworks and standards, considering the environmental and societal impacts, and promoting equitable access, these leaders can ensure that blockchain technology serves as a force for positive and sustainable societal advancement.

The growing concern over the environmental impact of blockchain technologies, especially the energy-intensive processes associated with certain cryptocurrencies, has underscored the urgent need for sustainable practices within this innovative field. As blockchain continues to evolve, the role of purpose-driven leaders becomes increasingly critical. These leaders are pivotal in steering the blockchain community towards more environmentally friendly practices and redefining what success looks like in the industry.

Purpose-driven leaders advocate for the adoption of energy-efficient consensus mechanisms such as proof-of-stake (PoS) or delegated proof-of-stake (DPoS), which significantly reduce the amount of energy required to maintain blockchain networks compared to the traditional proof-of-work (PoW) systems used by networks like Bitcoin. By promoting these less energy-intensive alternatives, these leaders not only address the immediate concerns of energy consumption but also help in making blockchain technology more sustainable in the long run.

Beyond promoting energy efficiency, purpose-driven leaders are also at the forefront of harnessing blockchain technology for environmental conservation projects. They support and initiate platforms that utilize blockchain for tracking renewable energy usage and trading carbon credits. Such initiatives can increase the transparency and efficiency of renewable energy markets, making it easier to verify the origin of green energy and to ensure that energy credits are not double-counted or fraudulently claimed. By providing a trustworthy and immutable record, blockchain can facilitate the growth of renewable energy adoption and help in the effective management and reduction of carbon footprints across industries. Furthermore, these leaders are actively involved in redefining the success metrics of the blockchain industry. Moving away from traditional measures that focus solely on profitability and technological advancements, they emphasize the importance of contributions towards environmental sustainability and social well-being. This shift in defining success encourages a more holistic approach to development and innovation in the blockchain space, promoting projects and practices that not only advance technological capabilities but also benefit the planet and its populations.

Incorporating these new metrics involves changing the conversation within the industry—from boardrooms to development teams—about what constitutes valuable innovation. It requires integrating sustainability goals into the core strategic objectives of blockchain enterprises. Purpose-driven leaders play a key role in this integration by advocating for policies and practices that align with environmental objectives, engaging with stakeholders to foster a shared commitment to sustainability, and driving investments towards projects that offer both economic and ecological benefits.

By championing these sustainable practices, purpose-driven leaders are not only mitigating the negative perceptions associated with blockchain technology but are also positioning it as a force for positive environmental change. Their efforts ensure that blockchain's potential is harnessed not just for economic disruption but also as a critical tool in the global fight against climate change, making the technology a cornerstone for future innovations that prioritize the health of our planet.

At the core of purpose-driven leadership in the blockchain and cryptocurrency sectors is a commitment to leveraging technology for social good. Leaders who embody this philosophy understand that technological advancements should not only solve technical problems but also address real-world issues, improve lives, and create a more equitable and sustainable world.

Such leaders are not content to merely ride the wave of technological disruption; they aim to direct this wave in ways that foster social change, ensure fair practices, and promote universal access to technology's benefits. Their vision and actions are crucial in ensuring that blockchain technology serves as a foundation for positive social transformation, aligning cutting-edge innovation with the pressing needs of our time.

The journey of blockchain as a tool for transformative social innovation is complex and fraught with challenges. However, the opportunities it presents for significant positive change are immense. With purpose-driven leadership at the helm, leveraging blockchain for social good can lead to profound and lasting impacts on society. Leaders in this space must navigate ethical dilemmas, advocate for responsible regulation, and ensure that technological advancements benefit all of society, especially those who are most vulnerable. By doing so, they will not only advance the technology but also shape the future of how blockchain impacts our world, making it more equitable, sustainable, and inclusive.

Integrating ethical decision-making into blockchain projects is crucial for fostering integrity and building stakeholder trust. Here are several strategies that leaders and developers can employ to ensure ethical practices are at the core of blockchain innovations.

Establishing clear ethical guidelines is crucial for ensuring that blockchain projects align with core Environmental, Social, and Governance (ESG) principles, particularly in areas like data privacy, user consent, transparency, and accountability. These guidelines serve as a cornerstone for decision-making, helping organizations navigate the complex ethical landscape of blockchain technology. For data privacy, ethical guidelines must clearly outline how personal and sensitive data will be handled, ensuring that it is collected, stored, and processed in ways that respect user privacy and comply with applicable laws. Moreover, obtaining user consent is paramount; guidelines should ensure that users are fully informed about what data is collected and how it will be used before they provide consent, which must be solicited in a straightforward and transparent manner to avoid coercion.

Transparency is another vital element in the ethical framework of blockchain projects. Organizations should leverage blockchain's inherent transparency to build trust among users and stakeholders by making operations clear and understandable. This ensures that users know how their data is used and how decisions are made within the blockchain ecosystem, balancing the need to protect sensitive information while maintaining transparency. Accountability is equally important. Ethical guidelines should include mechanisms for holding all participants, including developers, operators, and users, accountable for their actions. This accountability extends to implementing procedures for addressing misuse or unethical behavior and includes provisions for auditing and compliance checks to ensure adherence to the guidelines and proper operation of the system.

By defining what constitutes ethical behavior, organizations set a standard that all team members and stakeholders are expected to follow. These guidelines should be developed with input from a diverse group of experts, including ethicists, legal professionals, and blockchain developers, as well as representatives from the user base to ensure they are comprehensive and applicable. Additionally, these guidelines should be dynamic, evolving to address new challenges and ethical dilemmas as they arise.

Implementing such guidelines is not just about compliance; it's about fostering a culture of integrity and respect within the blockchain community. It involves educating team members and stakeholders about the importance of ethical standards and integrating them into daily decision-making processes. By prioritizing these ethical considerations, organizations can protect themselves from legal and reputational risks and contribute to making blockchain technology a force for positive societal change.

To ensure that blockchain projects adhere to established ethical standards, it is essential to implement rigorous compliance protocols. These protocols involve conducting regular audits and assessments to verify that all aspects of the project conform to both local and international laws and regulations. Compliance should not be treated as a one-time task but as an ongoing process that evolves in response to new legal developments and ethical considerations.

Regular audits are critical in identifying any deviations or lapses in adherence to ethical standards and regulatory requirements. These audits should be thorough and carried out by independent bodies when possible, to ensure objectivity and transparency. The findings from these audits can provide valuable insights into areas of the blockchain project that may require adjustments or enhancements to meet compliance standards.

Continuous monitoring of the regulatory landscape is crucial. As blockchain technology continues to advance and proliferate across different sectors, legal frameworks around the world are also evolving. Staying updated with these changes is vital for maintaining compliance, especially in a field as dynamic as blockchain. Projects may need to adapt to new regulations concerning data protection, financial transactions, or cross-border data flows, which could impact how blockchain networks are operated and managed.

Adapting to these legal developments requires a proactive approach to compliance. Blockchain projects should incorporate flexible frameworks that can quickly adjust to new regulatory requirements. This agility ensures that the project remains compliant and can continue operating without legal interruptions. Implementing rigorous compliance protocols also involves educating all participants about their responsibilities and the importance of adhering to ethical standards and regulations. Training sessions, regular updates, and clear communication channels can help ensure that everyone involved in a blockchain project understands the compliance requirements and the importance of their role in meeting these standards.

Compliance must be ingrained in the operational ethos of blockchain projects, with a clear strategy for ongoing monitoring, adaptation, and education. By taking these steps, blockchain initiatives can not only mitigate risks associated with non-compliance but also strengthen their credibility and trustworthiness in the eyes of users, regulators, and the broader community. This foundation of rigorous compliance not only protects the project and its users but also contributes to the broader goal of responsible and ethical innovation in the blockchain space.

Creating a culture that prioritizes ethical considerations within blockchain projects requires more than just establishing rules. It involves nurturing an environment where every team member, from developers to executives, understands and values the importance of ethics in their daily operations. This cultural shift is pivotal in ensuring that ethical practices are woven into the fabric of the organization and are reflected in every aspect of the project's lifecycle.

To achieve this, educational programs and workshops play a critical role. These initiatives can be instrumental in raising awareness about the ethical implications of blockchain technology and the specific challenges it may pose. For instance, training sessions can cover topics such as data privacy, the environmental impact of blockchain operations, the ethical use of artificial intelligence in smart contracts, and the socio-economic effects of deploying blockchain in various industries. By covering these topics, educational programs can equip team members with the knowledge and tools they need to identify and address ethical issues as they arise.

Workshops can provide practical, hands-on experience with ethical decision-making. Through interactive scenarios and role-playing exercises, team members can learn how to navigate complex ethical dilemmas that are common in the blockchain space. These activities encourage critical thinking and help individuals understand the often-nuanced nature of ethical decisions, particularly in a field as innovative and fast-paced as blockchain.

Regular discussions on ethical dilemmas related to blockchain are also crucial. These discussions can be facilitated through regular team meetings, dedicated forums, or digital platforms where team members can share their experiences, challenges, and insights. Encouraging open dialogue about ethical issues not only fosters a deeper understanding among team members but also helps to cultivate a mindset of continuous ethical improvement and vigilance. Such discussions should not be limited to hypothetical or past issues; they should also focus on proactive measures to anticipate and mitigate ethical risks. By regularly engaging with these topics, teams can stay ahead of potential ethical pitfalls and be better prepared to handle them effectively when they arise.

Fostering a culture of ethical awareness in blockchain projects requires commitment at all levels of the organization. Leadership must lead by example, demonstrating a commitment to ethical practices in their decision-making and interactions. At the same time, every team member should feel empowered and responsible for upholding the organization's ethical standards. This collective commitment can help ensure that the project not only succeeds in its technological and commercial goals but also contributes positively to society, adhering to the highest ethical standards.

Engaging stakeholders in discussions about the ethical implications of blockchain projects is crucial for maintaining transparency and building trust. By involving a diverse group of stakeholders—including customers, investors, regulatory bodies, community representatives, and industry experts—organizations can gather a wide range of perspectives that enrich the decision-making process. This proactive approach to stakeholder engagement helps to address concerns before they escalate and ensures that the blockchain project aligns with broader community and ethical standards.

One effective method of stakeholder engagement is through the organization of public forums. These forums provide a platform for open dialogue, allowing stakeholders to express their views, ask questions, and provide feedback on the project's development and its ethical considerations. Public forums not only foster transparency but also enhance the project's credibility by demonstrating the organization's commitment to ethical practices and community involvement.

Setting up stakeholder panels can be a strategic approach to continuous engagement. These panels, composed of a diverse group of stakeholders with varying expertise and interests, can meet regularly to review the project's progress and discuss ethical issues. The panels serve as a sounding board for the organization, offering insights and recommendations that can guide the project's ethical framework and operational strategies. This regular, structured engagement helps ensure that the project remains responsive to stakeholder concerns and adapts to changing expectations and ethical norms.

Regular updates and consultations are another key aspect of engaging stakeholders. Keeping stakeholders informed through newsletters, progress reports, and dedicated consultations helps maintain an open line of communication. These updates should provide clear and honest information about the project's achievements and challenges, particularly regarding ethical practices and decisions. Regular communication not only keeps stakeholders informed but also reinforces trust by showing that the organization values transparency and accountability.

Engaging stakeholders in this way encourages a sense of shared responsibility and collaboration. It allows stakeholders to feel part of the project's journey, which can lead to stronger support and a more committed relationship. Moreover, by actively involving stakeholders in ethical discussions, organizations can preemptively address potential issues, adapting their strategies to better meet the expectations and needs of the community and other interested parties. Stakeholder engagement is not just about gathering feedback; it's about building a collaborative environment where ethical standards are developed and upheld collectively. This approach not only enhances the project's ethical standing but also ensures that it delivers real value to both the organization and its wider community, fostering a sustainable and trusted blockchain initiative.

Transparency is indeed a cornerstone of ethical blockchain projects, playing a critical role in building and maintaining trust among all stakeholders involved. Developing robust mechanisms for transparent reporting is essential to keep stakeholders informed about project operations, progress, and decision-making processes. This transparency is not only a best practice but also a fundamental requirement in ensuring the accountability and integrity of blockchain initiatives.

One effective way to enhance transparency is through the publication of regular impact reports. These reports can provide comprehensive details about the project's achievements, challenges, and contributions to both economic and social goals. By documenting and sharing the outcomes and impacts of the project, organizations can demonstrate their commitment to transparency and ethical practices. Impact reports should ideally include quantitative metrics and qualitative assessments, offering a clear, balanced view of the project's performance and its alignment with stated objectives.

Updates on governance practices are also crucial for transparent reporting. Governance in blockchain projects involves the rules, procedures, and practices that dictate how decisions are made and how different stakeholders interact within the project. By regularly updating stakeholders on changes or developments in governance practices, organizations can ensure that all participants are aware of how decisions are being made, who is making them, and on what basis. This transparency in governance helps prevent misunderstandings and conflicts and fosters a collaborative environment. Disclosures of any conflicts of interest are vital to maintaining the ethical integrity of blockchain projects. Conflicts of interest, if not properly managed, can undermine trust and lead to decisions that might benefit a particular group at the expense of others. Transparent reporting should therefore include a clear disclosure of any potential or actual conflicts of interest among the project's leaders, developers, or other key stakeholders. This should be accompanied by an explanation of how these conflicts are being managed to ensure they do not adversely affect the project's outcomes or stakeholder interests. In addition to these specific reports, developing transparent reporting mechanisms might also involve leveraging the blockchain technology itself to enhance transparency. For example, organizations can use blockchain to create immutable records of key decisions, financial transactions, and contract fulfillments. These records can be made accessible to relevant stakeholders, providing a verifiable and tamper-proof audit trail that enhances the credibility and transparency of the project.

Engaging with stakeholders through interactive platforms where they can ask questions, provide feedback, and express concerns is another layer of transparency. These interactions can be facilitated through regular webinars, Q&A sessions, or open forums, fostering a two-way communication channel that emphasizes openness and responsiveness.

By implementing these comprehensive mechanisms for transparent reporting, blockchain projects can establish a strong foundation of trust and accountability, which is essential for long-term success and stakeholder support. This commitment to transparency not only aligns with ethical practices but also strengthens the project's reputation and efficacy in achieving its goals.

When designing blockchain systems, integrating ethical design principles is crucial for preventing misuse of technology and protecting user rights. This proactive approach involves considering the societal impacts of technology from the outset and deliberately designing solutions that promote privacy, security, and inclusivity.

Privacy and security are paramount in the design of blockchain systems. Developers must incorporate robust encryption methods and secure data handling practices to protect sensitive information from unauthorized access and potential breaches. Furthermore, privacy should be built into the design of the blockchain, ensuring that personal data is anonymized or securely encrypted to prevent potential misuse. This approach, often referred to as 'privacy by design', ensures that privacy measures are not mere add-ons but integral components of the blockchain system.

Blockchain systems should be designed with inclusivity in mind, ensuring that they are accessible to a wide range of users, including those with limited technical expertise or those from economically disadvantaged backgrounds. This involves creating user interfaces that are intuitive and easy to navigate, providing support and resources for users who may be less familiar with digital technologies, and ensuring that the technology does not require expensive or sophisticated hardware that could be a barrier to entry.

A critical aspect of ethical design in blockchain is ensuring that the technology does not exacerbate existing social and economic inequalities. For instance, while blockchain can provide enhanced access to financial services, designers must be wary of creating systems that require high levels of digital literacy or access to digital infrastructure, which might exclude large segments of the population. Instead, solutions should aim to bridge gaps in access and equity, perhaps by integrating features that cater to various levels of tech-saviness or by supporting multiple languages to broaden accessibility.

Ethical design also involves considering the long-term impacts of blockchain technology on society. This means thinking beyond the immediate benefits of the technology to understand how it might influence social structures, economic opportunities, and cultural norms over time. For example, the decentralization aspect of blockchain could shift power dynamics in many industries, from finance to media, potentially leading to significant societal changes. Designers must consider these potential impacts and strive to ensure that they contribute positively to societal development.

Employing ethical design principles in blockchain development often requires collaboration with a wide range of stakeholders, including ethicists, sociologists, potential users, and regulatory bodies. By engaging with these diverse groups during the design process, developers can gain valuable insights into the potential risks and ethical considerations associated with their projects. This collaborative approach can help identify unforeseen ethical dilemmas and ensure that the blockchain system is well-rounded and socially responsible. By integrating these ethical design principles, blockchain developers can create systems that not only leverage the technological strengths of blockchain but also actively contribute to building a fairer, more secure, and inclusive society. This commitment to ethical design will be crucial in fostering broader acceptance and success of blockchain technology in various societal applications.

Blockchain technology can serve as a powerful tool to enhance ethical practices within various systems. For instance, the integration of smart contracts can automate compliance checks and the enforcement of ethical guidelines, significantly reducing human error and bias. These smart contracts, when programmed correctly, execute automatically based on predefined conditions, ensuring that operations adhere to regulatory and ethical standards without the need for manual oversight. Additionally, blockchain's inherent attributes of immutability and transparency contribute to the creation of systems that stakeholders can trust. The unchangeable nature of blockchain ensures that once data has been entered, it cannot be altered, which prevents tampering and promotes accountability. Meanwhile, the transparency of blockchain systems means that all transactions are visible and traceable by all participants, enhancing the trustworthiness and auditability of the processes.

As the field of ethics in technology continues to evolve rapidly, it is crucial for leaders in blockchain to stay informed about the latest advancements in both technology and ethical standards. This involves not only keeping up with new technological innovations that can enhance the ethical implementation of blockchain projects but also staying updated on changes in societal expectations and ethical norms. Monitoring these developments allows leaders to adapt their practices effectively, integrating new insights and methodologies to address emerging ethical challenges.

Being adaptive is particularly important in the fast-paced realm of blockchain and technology. As new ethical dilemmas arise and societal expectations shift, blockchain projects must be ready to evolve. This might involve updating smart contracts to meet new ethical standards, incorporating more advanced security measures to protect user data, or reevaluating governance models to ensure they align with the latest best practices in corporate ethics.

Maintaining ethical integrity over time requires a proactive approach. Blockchain leaders should not only react to changes but anticipate them, engaging with ethical scholars, technology experts, and the broader community to foresee where adjustments might be needed in their systems. This forward-thinking approach ensures that blockchain technology continues to serve as a force for good, enhancing ethical practices across industries while adapting to the ever-changing landscape of technology and society.

Integrating ethical decision-making into blockchain projects is fundamental for ensuring that these technologies contribute positively to society and maintain stakeholder trust. By establishing clear guidelines, fostering a culture of ethics, engaging stakeholders, and leveraging technology, blockchain initiatives can uphold high ethical standards and lead by example in the tech world. As blockchain continues to evolve, maintaining a commitment to ethics will be essential for its sustainable and equitable growth, ensuring that it remains a force for good in addressing the world's most pressing challenges.

Chapter 6: Vision and Purpose: Guiding Blockchain Adoption

The importance of having clear vision and purpose statements in guiding blockchain initiatives cannot be overstated. These statements serve as a compass, directing the entire project from conception through to execution and beyond, ensuring that every effort is aligned with a central goal.

A well-articulated vision and purpose provide much-needed direction to a blockchain initiative. They help the team focus on specific objectives, guiding the actions needed to achieve them. This clarity prevents the project from veering off course, which can lead to wasted time and resources. It establishes a roadmap that the team can follow, making the process more efficient and goal-oriented. Beyond mere direction, a clear vision and purpose have the power to motivate and inspire those involved in the project. They imbue the team with a sense of meaning and commitment, making the work feel impactful and worthwhile. This can be particularly crucial during challenging phases of the project, where the intrinsic motivation derived from a compelling vision can drive the team to overcome obstacles.

These statements also enhance decision-making. With a defined purpose and vision, decisions can be evaluated based on whether they advance the project towards its stated goals. This framework helps in prioritizing resources and time effectively, ensuring that every action taken is strategic and contributes to the overarching objectives.

Accountability is another significant aspect influenced by a clear vision and purpose. When goals are explicitly stated, it becomes easier for the team to hold themselves accountable for reaching them. This accountability is essential for tracking progress and measuring success, allowing for adjustments and optimizations to be made in real time.

Moreover, a powerful vision and purpose statement can attract and secure the buy-in of crucial stakeholders. Investors, partners, and community members are more likely to support an initiative when its goals are compelling and its direction is clear. This external support is often critical for the successful implementation and scaling of blockchain projects.

Aligning the blockchain initiative's vision with the organization's overall business strategy is essential for sustaining long-term impact and value. This alignment ensures that the blockchain project supports and enhances the broader business objectives, integrating seamlessly into the organization's operational fabric.

Navigating regulatory landscapes is yet another area where clear vision and purpose prove beneficial. In contexts such as carbon accounting and emissions reporting, understanding the initiative's end goals can facilitate compliance with relevant regulations, making the process smoother and more efficient. Defining clear vision and purpose statements for blockchain initiatives is more than a procedural step; it's a strategic move that defines the project's trajectory and impact. These statements provide direction, inspire participation, guide decision-making, ensure accountability, attract stakeholder support, align with business strategies, and aid in regulatory compliance, collectively steering the project toward success.

Articulating the core values and vision of a blockchain initiative is essential for guiding its development and ensuring alignment with strategic goals. Below are effective exercises and strategies designed to define and communicate these foundational aspects comprehensively.

Organizing visioning workshops is a strategic approach to establishing a robust foundation for any blockchain initiative. By gathering key stakeholders such as founders, project managers, technical leads, and significant partners, these workshops create a collaborative environment where the long-term vision and aspirations of the project can be jointly developed and refined.

The process begins with scenario planning, a method that involves discussing various potential future scenarios in a structured manner. This part of the workshop encourages participants to think broadly and creatively about the range of possibilities for how the blockchain initiative might evolve over time. By considering different future contexts, including best-case and worst-case scenarios, stakeholders can identify opportunities and challenges that might not be immediately apparent. This foresight helps in crafting strategies that are resilient and adaptable to changes in the market or technology landscape.

Following scenario planning, the workshop typically transitions into storyboarding. This technique is used to visualize the project's journey and its future impact in a more tangible way. Storyboarding helps participants concretely outline the steps needed to achieve the envisioned future, turning abstract ideas into actionable strategies. By visually mapping out the project, stakeholders can see how different components of the initiative interact, where critical milestones lie, and how value will be delivered to users at each stage.

These visioning workshops are not only crucial for setting a clear and shared direction but also for ensuring alignment among all parties involved. When stakeholders have a common understanding of the project's goals and the path to achieving them, coordination becomes more straightforward, and the likelihood of conflicts or misalignments later in the project lifecycle is significantly reduced.

The collaborative nature of these workshops fosters a sense of ownership and commitment among the participants. When stakeholders are actively involved in shaping the vision, they are more likely to be invested in the success of the project and work cooperatively towards overcoming hurdles.

Visioning workshops serve as a vital tool in the strategic planning of blockchain initiatives. They provide a structured framework for imagining the future, crafting a shared vision, and planning the practical steps necessary to turn that vision into reality. This approach not only enhances the strategic alignment within the project team but also sets the stage for successful implementation and scaling of the blockchain initiative.

Brainstorming sessions dedicated to identifying core values are crucial for laying the ethical and operational foundation of any blockchain initiative. These sessions ensure that the values guiding the project resonate deeply with the beliefs and principles held by the team and the wider community they aim to serve. Such alignment is essential not only for internal coherence but also for building trust and rapport with external stakeholders and users. Employing techniques like mind mapping during these sessions can be particularly effective. Mind mapping is a visual organization tool that allows participants to branch out their thoughts from a central idea—in this case, the core values of the project. This method encourages a free flow of ideas, making it easier to explore and connect various concepts related to the values that should guide the blockchain initiative. The visual nature of mind maps helps clarify the relationships between different values and how they contribute to the overarching goals of the project.

In addition to mind mapping, it is beneficial to engage in exercises that focus on how the blockchain will create value for its users. Understanding the specific benefits that the blockchain will provide can lead to a more targeted and relevant set of core values. For example, if a blockchain project is focused on enhancing data security for users, values such as transparency, reliability, and integrity might be prioritized. Conversely, a project aimed at improving supply chain efficiencies might emphasize values like innovation, collaboration, and sustainability.

Outlining how the blockchain creates value for its users involves detailed discussions about the user experience, the problems being solved, and the improvements over existing solutions. This discussion should not only cover the technological aspects but also consider the social, economic, and environmental impacts of the blockchain project. By thoroughly understanding these elements, the team can derive a set of actionable and impactful values that truly resonate with both the project's goals and the needs of its users.

These brainstorming sessions should be inclusive, involving diverse viewpoints from various stakeholders. Including voices from different backgrounds and areas of expertise can enrich the discussion, ensuring that the core values are comprehensive and embrace a wider range of concerns and aspirations. This inclusivity strengthens the project's relevance and appeal to a broad audience.

Core values brainstorming sessions are a fundamental step in ensuring that a blockchain initiative is rooted in a strong ethical foundation that guides decision-making, shapes the technology's development, and influences how the project interacts with its community and stakeholders. These values become the bedrock upon which the project's culture and practices are built, influencing every aspect of the initiative from internal operations to user engagement and community relations.

Conducting interviews or organizing focus groups with a diverse range of stakeholders is an essential strategy for gathering external perspectives and ensuring that a blockchain initiative is aligned with the needs and expectations of its broader ecosystem. These stakeholders typically include potential users, regulatory bodies, industry experts, and other parties who might be affected by or have an interest in the project. The insights gained from these engagements are invaluable for refining the project's vision and ensuring its core values resonate with those it aims to serve.

The process of engaging stakeholders through interviews and focus groups involves several critical steps. Initially, identifying the right mix of stakeholders is crucial. This group should represent a cross-section of perspectives, including those from different geographic regions, industries, and professional backgrounds. By encompassing a broad spectrum of views, the project team can capture a comprehensive understanding of the varied expectations and concerns associated with the blockchain initiative.

During these interviews or focus groups, discussions should be structured to cover a wide range of topics. Key areas of focus include stakeholders' expectations of the blockchain project, their specific needs that the project could address, the benefits they perceive from using blockchain technology, and any concerns they might have about its implementation or broader impacts. These conversations should be open and exploratory, allowing stakeholders to express their thoughts freely, which can reveal new insights or highlight potential issues not previously considered by the project team. Potential users might provide practical insights into the usability and functionality of the blockchain system, suggesting features or identifying potential barriers to adoption. Regulatory bodies might highlight compliance challenges or suggest frameworks for ensuring the project meets legal standards. Industry experts could offer predictions on technology trends that could affect the project or advise on overcoming technical obstacles.

The information gathered from these interviews and focus groups should then be analyzed to identify common themes, priorities, and concerns. This analysis can help the project team to adjust the blockchain initiative's vision and redefine its core values to better align with stakeholder expectations. Additionally, these insights can guide the development of strategies to address stakeholder concerns, enhance user engagement, and ensure compliance with regulatory standards.

Stakeholder interviews and focus groups are not just about collecting data—they are about building relationships and trust with the community surrounding the blockchain project. Regular and meaningful engagement with stakeholders not only helps in aligning the project more closely with external expectations but also builds a foundation of support and advocacy that can be crucial for the project's success. This approach ensures that the blockchain initiative is grounded in a deep understanding of its ecosystem, enhancing its relevance, viability, and potential for positive impact.

Once the core values and vision of a blockchain initiative are firmly established, the next critical step is to articulate these elements through a strong mission statement. A well-crafted mission statement serves as a foundational communication tool that encapsulates the essence of what the blockchain initiative is set out to achieve. It plays a pivotal role in aligning internal objectives with external expectations, guiding decision-making, and fostering a shared understanding among all stakeholders.

A mission statement should be inspirational, capturing the imagination and commitment of everyone involved with or affected by the blockchain initiative. It should convey a sense of purpose and inspire stakeholders by clearly articulating the broader impact of the initiative. This could involve describing how the blockchain will revolutionize a particular industry, improve lives, or contribute to solving significant social or environmental challenges. The inspirational quality of the mission statement helps to motivate team members and stakeholders to work towards a common goal, providing a sense of purpose that transcends everyday tasks.

Alongside being inspirational, the mission statement must also be informative. It should provide clear and concise information about what the blockchain initiative does and how it intends to achieve its goals. This includes outlining the primary functions of the blockchain system, the key benefits it offers to users, and the strategies it will employ to meet its objectives. A precise mission statement helps to set clear expectations and serves as a guide for the initiative's strategic direction. It ensures that all stakeholders, from developers and investors to users and regulatory bodies, understand the initiative's focus and the means by which it will pursue its vision.

Developing such a mission statement involves a collaborative process where feedback from various stakeholders is incorporated.

This can be achieved through workshops, discussions, or surveys that invite stakeholders to contribute their views on what the initiative should aim to accomplish and how it should position itself in the broader market. This collaborative approach not only ensures that the mission statement is robust and comprehensive but also enhances buy-in from those involved, as they see their input reflected in the final statement.

It's crucial that the mission statement aligns with the previously established core values and vision of the initiative. This alignment ensures consistency in messaging and helps reinforce the principles that drive the blockchain project. The mission statement acts as a bridge between the strategic vision of the initiative and its operational activities, making sure that every action taken is guided by and contributes to the overarching goals.

The mission statement should be actively communicated and integrated into all aspects of the blockchain initiative. It should be visible in marketing materials, pitch presentations, internal communications, and strategic documents. More importantly, the mission should be lived daily by everyone involved in the project. Leaders should continuously reinforce the mission statement in their decisions and actions, embedding it into the organizational culture and practices. A strong mission statement not only succinctly communicates the purpose and direction of the blockchain initiative but also serves as a constant source of inspiration and alignment for all stakeholders involved. It encapsulates the aspirational and operational essence of the initiative, driving it forward with clarity and purpose.

Performing a SWOT analysis is a crucial strategic tool for any blockchain initiative, providing a clear framework to assess its internal capabilities and external environmental factors. This analysis helps in comprehensively understanding the strengths, weaknesses, opportunities, and threats related to the initiative, which is essential for aligning strategic planning with the initiative's vision and values.
The SWOT analysis begins by identifying the strengths of the blockchain initiative. These are the internal positive attributes and

resources that the initiative has at its disposal, which can include technological expertise, innovative solutions, a motivated team, strong leadership, or financial resources. Understanding these strengths allows the project to capitalize on what it does best, leveraging these assets to gain a competitive advantage or to strengthen its position in the market. For example, a blockchain initiative might have a particularly strong data security protocol that sets it apart from competitors, which could be highlighted and built upon.

The analysis also requires an honest assessment of the initiative's weaknesses. These are internal factors that might hinder the project's success or areas where the project lacks resources or capabilities. Weaknesses could include gaps in technical expertise, limited funding, operational inefficiencies, or lack of clear regulatory compliance strategies. Identifying these weaknesses is crucial as it allows the team to address and mitigate these issues before they impact the project's ability to achieve its goals.

Looking externally, the SWOT analysis identifies opportunities in the market that the blockchain initiative can exploit to its advantage. Opportunities can arise from a variety of sources such as technological advances, changes in regulations, market demands, or shifts in industry trends that the initiative can capitalize on. For instance, increasing global attention to privacy concerns might present an opportunity for a blockchain initiative focused on enhancing data privacy. The analysis examines the external threats that could pose challenges to the initiative. These might include competitive pressures, technological changes, adverse regulatory developments, or broader economic downturns. By anticipating potential threats, the initiative can develop strategies to cushion against these risks, ensuring greater resilience and adaptability in a rapidly changing environment.

Insights gained from the SWOT analysis are invaluable for the continuous refinement of the initiative's strategies and operations. This involves using the strengths to take full advantage of opportunities while also reinforcing areas of weakness against potential threats. For example, if the analysis reveals a strong technological base but a lack of user engagement, strategies might be developed to enhance marketing efforts or improve user interface design.

By regularly updating the SWOT analysis, the initiative can stay aligned with both internal changes and external developments. This ongoing process ensures that the initiative remains robust, agile, and capable of achieving its vision while upholding its core values in a dynamic market. This analytical approach not only guides the strategic direction but also embeds a culture of proactive assessment and adaptation within the organization.

Workshops dedicated to ensuring alignment across all aspects of a blockchain initiative are pivotal in maintaining coherence and integrity throughout the project's lifecycle. These alignment workshops are designed to bring various teams and stakeholders together — from technology development to marketing and customer support — to ensure that every operational facet of the initiative adheres to the defined vision and values.

One effective technique used in these workshops is role-play and simulations. This method allows participants to enact various operational scenarios to test how well different parts of the project align with the overarching vision and values. For example, a simulation might involve a scenario where the project faces a data breach or a sudden regulatory change. Participants would then role-play their responses and decision-making processes, providing insights into how prepared the initiative is to handle real-world challenges while staying true to its values. These exercises not only help in identifying potential misalignments but also encourage proactive thinking and problem-solving among team members. Another useful tool in these workshops is the creation of alignment matrices. These matrices help visualize how different project components — such as product features, business processes, or user policies — align with each core value of the initiative. Each element of the project is evaluated against criteria derived from the core values, and the degree of alignment is noted. This visual tool can highlight areas where the project excels in embodying its values and identify where improvements are needed. For instance, if "transparency" is a core value, the matrix can help assess how transparent each process within the project is, from code development to user data handling.

Interactive discussions during these workshops provide a platform for open communication between different teams. These discussions can uncover hidden challenges or opportunities for better integration of the project's values. For example, the technology team might share insights on how certain blockchain functionalities can enhance data security, aligning with the core value of "security." Marketing teams might explore how their strategies can better communicate the project's commitment to "fairness" or "equity."

Incorporating feedback mechanisms within these workshops is crucial. Feedback gathered from participants helps refine processes and strategies continually. This feedback loop ensures that as the project evolves, it remains aligned with the intended vision and values, adapting to new challenges and opportunities that arise. Alignment workshops should not be one-time events but part of an ongoing effort to maintain and reinforce the initiative's core values throughout its execution. Regularly scheduled workshops can keep all teams updated on any changes in the project's direction or external conditions, ensuring continuous alignment.

By conducting these comprehensive alignment workshops, blockchain initiatives can foster a unified approach that permeates all aspects of the project, enhancing team cohesion and project integrity. These workshops ensure that the initiative not only meets its technical and business objectives but also remains true to its foundational ethical commitments, ultimately leading to more sustainable and successful outcomes.

Developing a robust communication strategy is essential for any blockchain initiative aiming to maintain transparency and stakeholder engagement. This strategy ensures that the initiative's vision and values are clearly and consistently articulated across all channels, helping to align stakeholder expectations and foster a sense of community and partnership.

An effective communication strategy must include regular updates that keep all stakeholders informed about the project's developments and progress. Periodic newsletters are an excellent way to summarize recent developments, upcoming events, and general progress of the project, serving as a comprehensive touchpoint for stakeholders who prefer consolidated updates at regular intervals. Maintaining an active blog provides deeper insights into the project, exploring challenges, achievements, and the detailed stories behind the scenes, offering a platform for articulating thought leadership and technical breakthroughs. Social media platforms like Twitter, LinkedIn, Facebook, and Instagram facilitate real-time updates and engage a broader audience, allowing for interactive and immediate communication, making it ideal for announcing updates, sharing success stories, and promoting events.

To further enhance engagement, organizing webinars and workshops can be particularly effective. These events serve multiple purposes: they educate the community and stakeholders about blockchain technology and the specific applications of the initiative, crucial for demystifying the technology and making the project accessible to a non-technical audience. Interactive sessions such as Q&A segments allow stakeholders to ask questions, express concerns, and provide feedback directly to the project team, which is invaluable for adjusting the project's trajectory and operations to better meet the community's needs. Regularly scheduled webinars and workshops also help build a sense of community among stakeholders, fostering a collaborative environment where stakeholders feel valued and see themselves as active participants in the project's success.

The communication strategy should emphasize consistency and transparency. It's important that the messaging across all platforms remains consistent with the initiative's vision and values. This consistency helps to build trust and credibility over time. Transparency in communication—being open about challenges as well as celebrating milestones—encourages stakeholders to maintain their engagement and support for the project.

A successful communication strategy must be adaptable. As the blockchain initiative progresses, the strategy should evolve based on stakeholder feedback, changes in the market, and new goals of the project. Adapting the communication strategy ensures that it remains effective and relevant, keeping the stakeholder community well-informed and engaged throughout the lifecycle of the project. This strategy not only supports the project's objectives but also amplifies its impact by ensuring that all stakeholders are aligned and informed.

The exercises and strategies discussed in this chapter are foundational to more than just defining the core values and vision of a blockchain initiative; they are crucial for embedding these principles deeply into every layer of the project. From visioning workshops and core values brainstorming sessions to comprehensive SWOT analyses and alignment workshops, each activity is designed to ensure that the initiative's foundational principles are clearly understood and actively reflected in its daily operations and long-term strategies.

These structured exercises ensure that all team members and stakeholders are aligned with the project's goals, fostering a cohesive and collaborative environment. By consistently applying these strategies, a blockchain initiative can maintain its focus, adapt to new challenges, and remain resilient against external pressures. This foundational clarity is not just beneficial; it is essential for driving the project forward cohesively and securing its long-term success.

The integration of these exercises into the project's development process cultivates a strong, value-driven culture that propels the initiative toward achieving its objectives, ensuring that every strategic decision and technological development aligns with the overarching vision and core values. This alignment is what will differentiate the project in a competitive marketplace and enable it to deliver lasting impact, demonstrating the profound power of a well-grounded and thoroughly articulated blockchain initiative.

Chapter 7: Building Resilience in the Face of Blockchain Challenges

Blockchain technology, while revolutionary, brings with it inherent uncertainties and challenges that can test the resilience of both individuals and organizations involved. Developing resilience is therefore critical in navigating these challenges effectively and ensuring the long-term success of blockchain initiatives.

Understanding the unique challenges posed by blockchain technology is the first step in building resilience. These challenges include rapid technological changes, regulatory uncertainties, market volatility, and the complexities of securing decentralized networks. Recognizing these challenges early allows organizations to prepare more effectively and develop strategies to mitigate potential risks.

For individuals working within the blockchain space, fostering a resilient mindset is essential. This involves embracing a culture of continuous learning and adaptability. Given the rapid pace of technological advancement in blockchain, staying informed about the latest developments and being flexible enough to adapt to new information is crucial. A resilient mindset also includes the willingness to experiment and learn from failures, viewing them as opportunities for growth rather than setbacks.

At an organizational level, resilience can be bolstered through robust risk management strategies. This includes conducting thorough risk assessments to identify potential vulnerabilities in blockchain applications and implementing appropriate safeguards. Regularly updating these risk assessments as the project evolves is also essential to stay ahead of new challenges.

Resilience can be significantly enhanced by building a supportive community around blockchain initiatives. This community should include not only the project team but also stakeholders, users, and other partners who can offer support, share insights, and collaborate on solutions to common challenges. A strong community fosters a sense of belonging and collective responsibility, which can be invaluable during difficult times. Adopting agile methodologies can further enhance organizational resilience. Agile approaches allow teams to be more responsive to changes and uncertainties. By breaking down projects into smaller, manageable parts and using iterative development cycles, organizations can more easily adjust their strategies in response to feedback or changing conditions. Open communication is another pillar of resilience. Establishing transparent communication channels where team members can share concerns, provide feedback, and discuss challenges openly without fear of reprisal encourages problem-solving and helps prevent issues from escalating. Transparency with external stakeholders is also crucial to maintain trust and manage expectations effectively.

Given the evolving regulatory landscape surrounding blockchain, preparing for potential regulatory changes is a must. This involves staying informed about legislative developments in different jurisdictions and engaging with regulatory bodies. Being proactive in compliance can prevent disruptions and ensure the initiative remains on solid legal footing. Investing in continuous learning and development ensures that team members are equipped to handle the complexities of blockchain projects. Regular training sessions, workshops, and access to educational resources can keep the team skilled and knowledgeable, ready to tackle new challenges as they arise.

By developing personal and organizational resilience in these ways, those involved in blockchain initiatives can navigate the uncertainties of this dynamic field more effectively. Building resilience is not just about surviving in the face of challenges but thriving, enabling the project to grow and adapt over time. Building resilience in the realm of blockchain technology starts with a clear understanding of the inherent challenges that this innovative field presents. These challenges range from rapid technological changes and regulatory uncertainties to market volatility and the complexities of managing decentralized networks. Early recognition of these hurdles is crucial as it allows organizations to craft informed strategies and implement measures designed to mitigate potential risks effectively.

For individuals engaged in the blockchain sector, cultivating a resilient mindset is indispensable. This mindset revolves around embracing a culture of continuous learning and adaptability, which is essential given the fast-evolving nature of blockchain technology. Staying abreast of the latest developments and being agile enough to adapt to new information are critical skills in this dynamic field. Moreover, resilience involves developing the ability to experiment and embrace the learning opportunities that failures offer. Rather than viewing setbacks as purely negative experiences, a resilient mindset sees them as valuable steps in the learning process, each providing unique insights that contribute to personal and professional growth. This approach not only helps individuals to navigate the complexities of blockchain more effectively but also fosters a more innovative and responsive environment within organizations.

At the organizational level, building resilience within blockchain initiatives requires the implementation of robust risk management strategies. This process starts with conducting thorough risk assessments aimed at identifying potential vulnerabilities within blockchain applications. By pinpointing these vulnerabilities early, organizations can proactively address risks before they manifest into more significant issues.

To effectively manage these risks, appropriate safeguards must be established. These can include technical solutions such as enhanced cybersecurity measures, encryption techniques, and the implementation of multi-factor authentication systems to protect against unauthorized access. Additionally, operational safeguards such as clear policies and procedures for data handling, compliance checks, and regular security training for staff are crucial. These measures help ensure that every team member understands their role in maintaining the security and integrity of the blockchain system.

Because the landscape in which blockchain operates is continually evolving—marked by rapid technological advances and shifting regulatory environments—it is vital that risk assessments are not static. Organizations must commit to regularly updating their risk assessments to reflect new developments, discoveries, and external changes in the marketplace or regulatory frameworks. This ongoing process allows organizations to adapt their risk management strategies dynamically, ensuring they remain effective and relevant.

This proactive and adaptive approach to risk management not only mitigates immediate threats but also prepares organizations to better handle future challenges, thereby enhancing overall resilience. Through diligent and continuous risk assessment, coupled with the implementation of effective safeguards, blockchain projects can protect themselves against a wide array of risks, positioning them for long-term success and stability. Building a supportive community around blockchain initiatives plays a crucial role in enhancing the resilience of these projects. Such a community should extend beyond the immediate project team to include a diverse array of stakeholders, users, and partners. These community members bring a wealth of perspectives, experiences, and expertise that can contribute significantly to the project's success.

The benefits of fostering a strong community are manifold. Firstly, a well-engaged community offers support not just in terms of project development and execution but also during setbacks and challenges. Community members can provide practical solutions, offer moral support, and share their own experiences of overcoming similar obstacles. This collective wisdom and encouragement are vital during difficult times, helping to sustain momentum and morale. A supportive community facilitates open communication and collaboration, allowing for the exchange of ideas and insights that can drive innovation and improve project outcomes. For instance, regular community meetups, online forums, and collaborative workshops can serve as platforms where stakeholders can voice concerns, propose enhancements, and share best practices. This ongoing dialogue ensures that the project remains responsive to the needs and expectations of its user base and is adaptable to the changing dynamics of the blockchain ecosystem.

A strong community also instills a sense of belonging and collective responsibility among its members. When stakeholders feel they are part of a larger effort and see their input valued, they are more likely to invest not just their time and resources but also their loyalty and advocacy for the project. This sense of ownership can be a powerful motivator, driving community members to contribute actively to the project's success. Community-building initiatives such as educational programs, volunteer opportunities, and community-led projects can enhance engagement and empowerment. By involving community members in these activities, blockchain initiatives can harness their skills and enthusiasm for mutual benefit. For example, user-led tutorials or stakeholder panels can help demystify blockchain technology and encourage wider participation and adoption.

The resilience of blockchain initiatives is greatly enhanced by the presence of a supportive community. Such a community not only provides a safety net during challenges but also serves as a dynamic resource for innovation and growth. By actively building and nurturing these relationships, blockchain projects can create a robust ecosystem that is well-equipped to thrive in the ever-evolving technological landscape.

Adopting agile methodologies is an effective strategy for enhancing organizational resilience, particularly in the fast-paced and often unpredictable world of blockchain technology. Agile approaches enable teams to be highly responsive to changes and uncertainties, which are commonplace in emerging technological fields. Agile methodologies are characterized by their flexibility and adaptability. They involve breaking down large projects into smaller, more manageable parts, known as iterations or sprints. This modular approach allows teams to focus on developing one aspect of a project at a time, making it easier to incorporate changes or pivot directions based on new information or feedback without disrupting the entire project's progress.

Each iteration in an agile methodology typically includes stages of planning, development, testing, and review. This cyclical process ensures that at the end of each iteration, a working part of the project is completed and can be evaluated by the team. The iterative development cycles encourage continuous improvement and allow for regular assessment of the project's alignment with user needs and market demands.

The use of iterative cycles also facilitates a consistent feedback loop with stakeholders, including users, investors, and regulatory bodies. By regularly presenting them with tangible outputs, organizations can gather valuable insights and constructive criticisms that can be used to refine the project. This ongoing engagement not only helps in building a product that truly resonates with its audience but also strengthens stakeholder relationships by making them feel involved in the development process.

Agile methodologies promote a dynamic work environment that can rapidly adapt to external changes. Whether these changes stem from technological advancements, competitive pressures, or regulatory updates, agile teams can quickly integrate these considerations into their project workflows. This responsiveness is crucial for maintaining relevance and competitiveness in the blockchain space, where new developments and adjustments are frequent. Agile practices encourage collaboration and transparency within teams. Daily stand-ups, sprint reviews, and retrospective meetings keep team members aligned on project goals, tasks, and challenges. This open communication helps identify bottlenecks early, spreads knowledge across the team, and ensures that everyone is on the same page, contributing to a more cohesive and efficient working environment.

Leveraging agile methodologies not only enhances an organization's ability to adapt to changes and feedback efficiently but also fosters a proactive, inclusive, and collaborative culture. This adaptability and team cohesion are essential for building resilience in the blockchain arena, enabling organizations to navigate the complexities of this dynamic field successfully and sustain long-term growth.

Encouraging open communication within a blockchain initiative is fundamental to building a resilient organization. By establishing transparent communication channels, teams can foster an environment where concerns and challenges can be shared openly, without fear of reprisal. This transparency is crucial for effective problem-solving and helps prevent minor issues from escalating into major setbacks. Regular meetings, feedback sessions, and open forums can be instrumental in creating these open lines of communication. Additionally, using digital tools that facilitate real-time sharing and collaboration can enhance transparency and ensure that all team members are on the same page, regardless of their physical location.

Maintaining open communication with external stakeholders—such as investors, customers, and regulatory authorities—is equally important. It helps manage expectations by keeping stakeholders informed about the project's progress, challenges, and changes. Transparency with stakeholders not only builds trust but also garners broader support, as stakeholders feel more connected and involved in the project's journey. Regular updates through newsletters, stakeholder meetings, and public reports are ways to ensure that the communication remains consistent and engaging.

Preparing for regulatory shifts is another critical aspect of resilience in blockchain initiatives. The regulatory landscape for blockchain is still evolving, with many jurisdictions working to establish frameworks that balance innovation with risk management. Staying informed about these legislative developments is imperative for any blockchain project. This means regularly monitoring legal changes, participating in industry forums, and perhaps even engaging legal experts or consultants who specialize in blockchain regulation.

Engagement with regulatory bodies is also a proactive strategy that can significantly benefit blockchain initiatives. By maintaining open lines of communication with regulators, organizations can gain insights into potential regulatory changes before they are formally implemented, allowing for smoother adaptation. Proactive compliance efforts, such as conducting internal audits and ensuring all operations are in line with current laws, can mitigate the risk of legal challenges and disruptions. This readiness not only protects the project legally but also reinforces its credibility and reliability in the eyes of stakeholders and the public.

Investing in continuous learning and development is crucial for maintaining the agility and effectiveness of teams working on blockchain projects. As blockchain technology continues to evolve rapidly, the skills and knowledge required to navigate this field also change. By prioritizing continuous learning, organizations can ensure that their team members are well-prepared to handle the complexities and dynamics of blockchain initiatives.

Regular training sessions play a vital role in this continuous learning landscape. These sessions can be tailored to cover new technological advancements, emerging industry trends, or changes in regulatory frameworks affecting blockchain technology. By keeping the team updated through these structured learning opportunities, organizations can foster a workforce that is both versatile and proficient.

Workshops offer another excellent avenue for development, providing hands-on experiences where team members can apply new skills in practical settings. Workshops can focus on specific areas such as smart contract development, blockchain security practices, or even soft skills like project management and cross-functional communication. These interactive sessions not only enhance technical proficiency but also encourage problem-solving and innovative thinking.

Access to a variety of educational resources further supplements the learning environment. This can include subscriptions to industry publications, online courses from reputable platforms, and participation in blockchain conferences and seminars. Such resources provide team members with a broader perspective of the blockchain ecosystem, exposing them to cutting-edge ideas and debates that can spark innovation within their own projects.

Creating an internal knowledge-sharing culture can amplify learning outcomes. Encouraging team members to share insights, discoveries, and lessons learned from their own experiences can lead to a more informed and engaged team. Internal presentations, lunch-and-learn sessions, and collaborative projects are effective ways to facilitate this exchange of knowledge. Investing in continuous learning and development is not just about keeping up with industry standards but also about empowering team members to excel in their roles. It prepares them to tackle new challenges head-on and with confidence, ensuring the organization not only adapts but thrives in the ever-changing landscape of blockchain technology.

We explored various strategies and practices essential for developing both personal and organizational resilience in the context of blockchain initiatives. As we've seen, resilience is crucial for navigating the inherent uncertainties and rapid changes characteristic of the blockchain field. By understanding the unique challenges posed by blockchain technology, such as rapid technological evolution, regulatory flux, and market volatility, organizations can better prepare to mitigate risks and adapt to new developments. We also discussed the importance of fostering a resilient mindset among individuals within the blockchain space, emphasizing continuous learning, adaptability, and the capacity to view setbacks as growth opportunities. Organizational resilience is reinforced through robust risk management strategies, which involve regular assessments and the implementation of appropriate safeguards to protect against vulnerabilities.

Building a supportive community around blockchain initiatives enhances resilience by providing a network of collaboration and support, which is invaluable during challenges. Adopting agile methodologies allows organizations to remain flexible and responsive to change, ensuring they can quickly adjust their strategies in response to feedback or evolving conditions. Open communication and transparency with all stakeholders, including team members and external partners, are vital for fostering an environment where challenges can be addressed openly and efficiently.

Preparing for regulatory shifts by staying informed and engaged with the evolving legal landscape helps ensure that blockchain projects remain compliant and sustainable over the long term. Lastly, investing in continuous learning and development ensures that team members remain knowledgeable and skilled, ready to tackle new challenges as they arise.

By implementing these strategies, those involved in blockchain initiatives can do more than just survive; they can thrive. Building resilience enables projects to grow, evolve, and adapt over time, turning potential obstacles into opportunities for innovation and success. This dynamic approach not only sustains the project through immediate challenges but also positions it for long-term achievement in the ever-evolving world of blockchain technology.

Chapter 8: Leading Through Change and Fostering Adaptability Within the Blockchain Ecosystem

In the dynamic realm of blockchain technology, the capacity to effectively lead through change and foster adaptability is not just advantageous—it's essential. As blockchain continues to disrupt traditional industries and reshape business landscapes, leaders within this space are tasked with guiding their teams through not only technological shifts but also the accompanying cultural and procedural transformations. This chapter will explore how effective leadership can drive adaptability and manage the constant flux inherent in the blockchain ecosystem.

Leaders in the blockchain industry must embody a visionary mindset. They need to possess a deep understanding of the current landscape while also anticipating future trends and challenges that might impact their projects. This type of foresight is critical, as it enables leaders to proactively steer their teams and projects, preparing strategically for potential shifts rather than merely reacting to them. Visionary leadership involves articulating a clear, compelling vision for the future that aligns with both the transformative potential of blockchain technology and the evolving demands of the market.

Agility is another cornerstone of effective leadership in the blockchain sector, characterized by rapid technological advancements and frequent market shifts. Leaders must foster an organizational culture that embraces change as a constant and views agility as a fundamental competency. This entails implementing flexible processes and organizational structures that can swiftly respond to new information, market changes, or technological developments. Agile leadership also encourages teams to adopt a mindset of experimentation and iterative learning, enabling them to refine strategies and operations continuously based on real-world feedback and results.

Given the fast-paced evolution of blockchain technology, continuous learning is crucial for maintaining relevance and competitiveness. Leaders should champion a learning-oriented environment where ongoing education and professional development are prioritized. Providing team members with access to the latest training, as well as opportunities to attend blockchain-related forums, workshops, and conferences, helps to keep the organization at the forefront of industry developments and best practices. This not only enhances the team's expertise but also fosters a proactive approach to innovation and problem-solving.

Blockchain inherently supports decentralized and collaborative approaches. Effective leaders capitalize on this aspect by developing collaborative ecosystems that encompass a variety of stakeholders, including developers, investors, business partners, and even competitors. Such ecosystems are invaluable for facilitating the exchange of ideas, pooling resources, and driving collective innovation. Leaders must create and maintain networks characterized by open communication and mutual support, fostering a collaborative culture that can dynamically adapt to new challenges and opportunities.

Strategic planning within a blockchain-focused organization must also be adaptive. Leaders should utilize planning techniques that allow for flexibility and responsiveness to changing conditions. This might involve adopting shorter strategic cycles or designing strategies that are modular and can be easily adjusted as external conditions dictate. By maintaining strategic flexibility, leaders can ensure that their organizations remain aligned with both immediate realities and long-term objectives.

Blockchain projects often face unexpected challenges and setbacks. Leaders must cultivate resilience and flexibility within their teams, encouraging them to view failures as learning opportunities and to persist in the face of difficulties. Developing a team's capacity to adapt its strategies or operational approaches when necessary is crucial for navigating the uncertainties of the blockchain landscape.

Leading effectively through the multifaceted changes characteristic of the blockchain ecosystem demands a blend of visionary insight, operational agility, continuous learning, collaborative engagement, adaptive strategic planning, and a strong emphasis on resilience and flexibility. By embracing these leadership qualities, those at the helm of blockchain initiatives can ensure that their organizations are not only prepared to manage current changes but are also well-equipped to thrive in the future landscape of this promising technological frontier. In the rapidly evolving blockchain industry, visionary leadership is not merely an asset; it is a necessity. Leaders within this space must possess an insightful understanding of both the current landscape and the potential future developments that could shape their sector. This foresight is crucial as it equips leaders to navigate not just immediate challenges but also to strategically position their projects for upcoming opportunities and shifts in the technological, economic, and regulatory environments.

Visionary leaders in blockchain distinguish themselves by their ability to anticipate and prepare for future trends and challenges. This proactive approach ensures that their teams and projects are not caught off-guard by changes but are ready to leverage new opportunities as they arise. For example, a leader might foresee the implications of new privacy regulations and adapt their blockchain project accordingly before these regulations become law, thereby securing a competitive advantage and ensuring compliance. Visionary leadership extends beyond mere anticipation. It involves articulating a clear and compelling vision of the future that motivates and unifies the team and stakeholders. This vision must align with the vast potential of blockchain technology while also resonating with the evolving needs of the market. For instance, if a blockchain leader envisions a platform that drastically reduces transaction costs for remittances, they must communicate how this aligns with broader financial accessibility goals and market demand for cheaper, faster financial services.

Such leaders use their vision as a strategic compass, guiding all aspects of the project—from product development to marketing strategy, stakeholder engagement, and beyond. They ensure that every team member understands and shares the vision, fostering a cohesive effort towards common goals. This shared vision helps maintain alignment and motivation across the organization, even as the project scales or pivots in response to new challenges. Visionary leadership in blockchain involves continuous engagement with emerging technologies and market trends. Leaders must stay well-informed about advancements not only within blockchain but also in related fields like artificial intelligence, cybersecurity, and the Internet of Things. This broad technological awareness enables them to identify synergies that can enhance their projects and foresee disruptions that could threaten their viability.

Visionary leadership in the blockchain space demands a blend of strategic foresight, clear communication, and dynamic adaptation. Leaders who embody these qualities can effectively steer their projects through the complexities of today's digital economy, ensuring their initiatives not only survive but thrive in the ever-changing landscape of blockchain technology.

In the blockchain sector, where technological advancements occur at a breakneck pace, cultivating a culture of agility is essential for any organization aiming to remain competitive and innovative. Agility in this context goes beyond mere flexibility; it requires an organizational culture that not only anticipates change but also embraces it as a regular aspect of daily operations. For leaders in the blockchain space, this means fostering an environment where agility is viewed as a core competency, integral to the organization's approach to all its activities.

Implementing flexible processes and structures is a key component of cultivating this agile culture. Leaders must design their organizational frameworks to be adaptable, allowing for quick adjustments in response to new information, technological updates, or shifts in market conditions. This might include adopting modular project management approaches that allow different teams to work on discrete components of a project that can easily be adjusted or reconfigured without disrupting the entire system. Such structures empower teams to respond swiftly and effectively, turning potential challenges into opportunities for growth and learning.

Agile leadership involves a strong emphasis on experimentation and iterative development. Leaders should encourage their teams to try new ideas and explore innovative solutions without the fear of failure. This experimental mindset should be supported by processes that allow for rapid prototyping, testing, and refinement of ideas. Each iteration provides valuable lessons and insights, which are critical for the continuous improvement of processes and products. Encouraging teams to iterate and learn from each trial involves creating a supportive environment where mistakes are seen as a natural part of the learning process. This approach not only accelerates innovation but also helps build a resilient team that is capable of handling the uncertainties inherent in the blockchain industry. By fostering a culture where feedback is actively sought and valued, leaders can ensure that learning is integrated into the fabric of the organization's operations.

In addition to internal processes, cultivating agility also means staying connected with the external environment. Leaders should ensure that their teams are not working in silos but are actively engaged with the wider blockchain community, industry trends, and customer feedback. This openness enhances the organization's ability to anticipate market needs and adapt products or services before competitors do, thereby maintaining a strategic edge.

Cultivating a culture of agility within a blockchain organization requires leaders to champion adaptability and continuous improvement. By implementing flexible organizational structures, encouraging iterative learning, and promoting active engagement with both internal and external environments, leaders can ensure that their teams are not only prepared to meet the current demands of the blockchain industry but are also equipped to lead its future development.

In the fast-paced and ever-evolving blockchain industry, continuous learning is not just beneficial—it's a necessity for staying competitive and innovative. Leaders within this field have a critical role in fostering an environment where education and skill development are prioritized. By promoting continuous learning, leaders ensure that their teams remain on the cutting edge of technology, well-informed about the latest industry trends, and aware of regulatory changes that could impact their projects.

One effective way to promote ongoing education is by providing regular access to training and professional development opportunities. This can include in-house training sessions led by knowledgeable staff or external experts, online courses from established educational platforms specializing in blockchain and related technologies, and regular updates on industry standards and best practices. Such initiatives ensure that team members' skills and knowledge are continuously updated, allowing them to tackle new challenges with confidence and expertise. Leaders should encourage participation in professional forums, workshops, and conferences.

These events serve as valuable platforms for learning from thought leaders, sharing experiences with peers, and exploring new ideas and technologies. They also provide networking opportunities that can lead to collaborations and partnerships, further enhancing the team's capabilities and reach. Engagement in these professional settings helps team members gain insights into how different organizations handle similar challenges and stay informed about technological and regulatory developments globally. In addition to formal training and networking, promoting a culture of informal learning and knowledge sharing within the organization is also beneficial. This can be facilitated through regular tech talks, where team members present interesting findings, new technologies, or lessons learned from recent projects to their colleagues. Establishing internal message boards or digital forums where employees can post articles, ask questions, and share insights can also promote an ongoing dialogue around continuous improvement and learning.

Leaders can encourage a mentorship culture where more experienced employees guide newcomers or less experienced staff through the complexities of blockchain technology and projects. This not only helps newer team members ramp up faster but also reinforces the knowledge and leadership skills of mentors, creating a mutually beneficial learning environment. By embedding continuous learning into the organizational culture, leaders in the blockchain field can cultivate a team that is resilient, adaptable, and equipped to drive innovation. This approach ensures that the organization not only keeps pace with the industry's rapid developments but also leads in shaping its future.

Blockchain technology's inherent qualities of decentralization and transparency naturally foster environments that thrive on collaboration. Recognizing this, effective leaders in the blockchain space actively work to create and sustain collaborative ecosystems that extend beyond their immediate teams to include a wide array of stakeholders—developers, investors, business partners, academic institutions, and regulatory bodies. This comprehensive approach to collaboration is crucial as it enriches the project with diverse perspectives and expertise, enhancing the overall innovation and adaptability of the organization.

To cultivate these collaborative ecosystems, leaders must first establish and maintain open lines of communication. This ensures that all participants can share ideas, voice concerns, and offer feedback freely and without barriers. Open communication fosters a culture of trust and transparency, which are essential for successful collaboration, especially in fields as complex and rapidly evolving as blockchain technology.

Creating formal and informal networks where stakeholders can interact and exchange information is vital. This might involve setting up regular networking events, online forums, collaborative workshops, and think tanks that bring together diverse groups to brainstorm solutions to common challenges. These interactions not only spur innovation but also strengthen relationships between different actors in the ecosystem, making it easier to collaborate effectively on projects.

Leaders should also focus on mutual support within these ecosystems. This involves recognizing and aligning the different but complementary strengths of each participant. For example, developers might have deep technical knowledge, while investors might offer insights into market dynamics and business scaling. By facilitating a platform where these diverse strengths can be utilized effectively, leaders can drive their projects forward more efficiently. Moreover, embracing tools and technologies that enhance collaborative efforts is another key strategy. Utilizing collaborative software, shared digital workspaces, and blockchain itself as a tool for collaboration can help streamline processes and enhance the productivity of the ecosystem. These technologies make it easier to manage projects, share documents securely, and maintain transparent records of collaborations and transactions.

Effective leaders also ensure that these ecosystems are inclusive, inviting participation from underrepresented groups and new entrants to the blockchain field. This inclusivity not only broadens the range of ideas and experiences within the ecosystem but also helps build a more robust and resilient blockchain community.

In fostering these collaborative ecosystems, leaders not only amplify the impact of their own projects but also contribute to the growth and sustainability of the blockchain industry as a whole. By encouraging knowledge sharing, innovation, and mutual support, they enable their organizations to adapt more fluidly to changes and challenges, securing a competitive edge in this dynamic field.

Implementing adaptive strategic planning is crucial for blockchain organizations due to the rapid pace of change and uncertainty inherent in the technology and its applications. Adaptive strategic planning ensures that an organization can pivot and evolve its strategies to meet the shifting demands of the market and the regulatory environment, thereby maintaining relevance and competitiveness.

Leaders in the blockchain space can start by incorporating adaptive planning techniques that prioritize flexibility and responsiveness. One effective approach is to set shorter strategic cycles. Traditional long-term planning may not be suitable in industries like blockchain, where technological and market conditions can change drastically in a short period. By shortening strategic cycles, organizations can evaluate their progress more frequently and make timely adjustments to their strategies. This iterative process allows leaders to refine their approach continuously based on the latest data and feedback.

Another strategy is to create modular strategic plans. This involves developing components of the strategy that can be quickly reconfigured or recombined in response to new information or changes in the environment. Modular planning allows an organization to adapt parts of its strategy without needing to overhaul the entire plan, thus enabling more agile responses to unexpected challenges or opportunities. This kind of planning should include mechanisms for real-time feedback collection from various sources—customers, partners, internal teams, and market analysts. This feedback is invaluable as it provides direct insights into how well the strategies are working and what adjustments might be necessary. Incorporating this feedback into the strategic planning process ensures that the organization remains aligned with user needs and market trends.

Leaders should also employ scenario planning as part of their strategic toolkit. Scenario planning involves envisioning different future scenarios based on current trends and potential changes in the environment, such as new technological developments, policy changes, or shifts in consumer behavior. By preparing strategies that address these various potential scenarios, a blockchain organization can react more swiftly and effectively when similar situations arise in reality.

Leveraging data analytics and predictive modeling can enhance the adaptability of strategic planning. These tools can help leaders anticipate market trends, identify emerging opportunities, and predict potential risks before they become evident. Armed with this information, organizations can preemptively adjust their strategies to seize opportunities or mitigate risks. Adaptive strategic planning is a dynamic approach that requires ongoing attention and refinement. It involves setting shorter planning cycles, creating modular strategies, utilizing real-time feedback, engaging in scenario planning, and applying advanced analytics. By embracing these practices, leaders of blockchain organizations can ensure that their strategies are as agile and resilient as the technologies they work with, positioning them to thrive in an ever-changing landscape.

Encouraging resilience and flexibility within teams is critical for navigating the often-unpredictable journey of blockchain projects. Blockchain initiatives frequently encounter unexpected challenges and setbacks due to the emerging nature of the technology, rapidly changing regulatory landscapes, and volatile market conditions. Effective leaders recognize the importance of fostering an environment where resilience and flexibility are not just encouraged but are integral components of the organizational culture.

Resilience in the context of blockchain projects involves cultivating the ability within team members to withstand setbacks and recover quickly from failures. This kind of resilience is crucial because it enables individuals and teams to maintain their momentum and continue pushing forward despite difficulties. Leaders can foster resilience by creating a supportive work environment that views failures as opportunities for learning and growth. This can be achieved by openly discussing setbacks as part of the learning process during team meetings, sharing lessons learned, and recognizing individuals who demonstrate perseverance and the ability to overcome difficulties.

Flexibility, on the other hand, refers to the capacity of individuals and the organization as a whole to adapt strategies or operational approaches in response to new information or changing circumstances. In the fast-evolving blockchain environment, the ability to pivot quickly can be a significant competitive advantage.

Leaders can encourage flexibility by implementing agile methodologies that allow for rapid iteration and adjustment of plans based on feedback and changing conditions. This might involve flexible project management practices that accommodate changes without disrupting the overall flow of work. To truly embed resilience and flexibility within a blockchain organization, leaders should also focus on training and development programs that emphasize these traits. Workshops on adaptive thinking, problem-solving in high-pressure situations, and effective change management can equip team members with the skills they need to adapt and thrive in a dynamic environment. Additionally, fostering a culture of open communication helps ensure that team members feel comfortable sharing their ideas for improvement and innovation, further enhancing the organization's flexibility.

Recognizing and rewarding resilience and flexibility can reinforce their value within the team. Leaders can acknowledge and reward behaviors that demonstrate adaptability and perseverance through formal recognition programs or informal praise in team settings. This not only motivates individuals to continue exhibiting these traits but also sets a precedent for others in the organization.

Encouraging resilience and flexibility is vital for leaders in the blockchain space. By fostering these qualities, leaders can help their teams navigate the complexities of blockchain projects more effectively, enabling them to not just survive but thrive amidst the challenges and capitalize on the opportunities that arise. This approach ensures that the organization remains robust and agile, ready to face whatever the future holds with confidence.

Engaging with the global blockchain community is an essential strategy for leaders who aim to keep their blockchain initiatives innovative, relevant, and competitive. Blockchain technology does not exist in isolation; it is a dynamic, globally interconnected field where developments in one part of the world can have ripple effects across the entire industry. Effective leaders understand the importance of tapping into this global network to gather diverse insights, stay abreast of emerging trends, and foster collaborative relationships.

Participation in the global blockchain community allows leaders and their teams to observe firsthand how blockchain technologies are being applied in different cultural and regulatory environments. This exposure can unveil unique use cases and creative implementations that may not be apparent or feasible in one's immediate surroundings. For instance, blockchain applications in supply chain management may vary significantly between Asia, Europe, and North America due to differing regulatory standards and market needs. Understanding these variations can inspire adaptations and innovations that enhance a project's applicability and scalability across borders.

Engaging with the global community helps leaders to identify and understand emerging best practices and technological advancements. The blockchain field is continually evolving, with new developments in areas like security protocols, consensus algorithms, and smart contract design occurring regularly. By connecting with peers worldwide, leaders can exchange knowledge and experiences that contribute to a collective advancement of the field. Such engagements often take place in international conferences, specialized webinars, and collaborative research projects.

The global blockchain community is a rich source of potential partnerships and collaborations. Blockchain projects often benefit from cross-border collaborations that combine diverse skill sets, resources, and market insights. Through active participation in global forums and networks, leaders can find partners whose strengths complement their own, facilitating joint ventures that can accelerate project development and enhance market reach.

Leaders can also leverage global engagement to advocate for favorable regulatory frameworks and standards that facilitate international cooperation and innovation in blockchain technology. By participating in policy discussions and regulatory forums, leaders can help shape the policies that will govern the future of blockchain technology, ensuring they are conducive to growth and innovation.

Engaging with the global blockchain community is not just about staying informed or building networks; it's about actively participating in the shaping of the blockchain landscape. By understanding how blockchain is evolving globally, adopting emerging best practices, fostering international collaborations, and influencing policy, leaders can ensure their projects are not only locally successful but also globally resonant and impactful.

Leading effectively through the myriad changes in the blockchain ecosystem demands a comprehensive and adaptable approach. Visionary leadership is essential, providing the foresight and direction needed to navigate the future landscape of blockchain technology. Such leaders not only anticipate emerging trends and potential challenges but also inspire their teams and stakeholders with a compelling vision of what can be achieved. Visionary leadership alone is not enough. It must be coupled with a culture of agility—an environment that embraces rapid change as a constant and sees adaptability as a critical competency. This agility enables organizations to pivot quickly in response to new information, technological advancements, or shifts in market dynamics, ensuring they remain relevant and competitive.

Continuous learning is another pillar of effective leadership in the blockchain space. As the technology and its applications evolve, so too must the skills and knowledge of those who work with it. Leaders must champion an environment where learning is continuous and integrated into the daily activities of the team, providing training and development opportunities that keep pace with industry advancements. Strategic adaptability further underpins the ability to lead through change. Adaptive strategic planning, which incorporates real-time feedback and allows for iterative adjustments, ensures that organizations can respond swiftly to changes without losing sight of their long-term goals.

By integrating these key elements—visionary leadership, cultural agility, continuous learning, and strategic adaptability—leaders can create an environment that not only withstands the turbulence of the present but is also well-equipped to handle the uncertainties of the future. This holistic approach to leadership ensures that blockchain initiatives are robust, responsive, and ready to capitalize on the opportunities of a rapidly evolving digital landscape. Ultimately, these leadership qualities are what will define the success and sustainability of blockchain initiatives in a complex and ever-changing world.

Chapter 9: Communicating the Impact: Blockchain and ESG Narratives

Effective communication is crucial for conveying the achievements and challenges of blockchain initiatives, especially in the realm of Environmental, Social, and Governance (ESG) goals. Transparent and impactful communication strategies not only demonstrate the value and progress of blockchain projects but also build trust and engagement among stakeholders. Here's how organizations can craft compelling narratives around their blockchain and ESG initiatives.

Crafting a compelling story is a fundamental aspect of effective communication, particularly when conveying the complexities and nuances of blockchain initiatives aimed at achieving Environmental, Social, and Governance (ESG) goals. A well-crafted narrative serves as a bridge between the technical aspects of blockchain technology and its real-world impacts, making the initiative accessible and engaging to a broader audience.

The story must clearly articulate how the blockchain initiative aligns with specific ESG objectives. This involves identifying and detailing the direct benefits that the technology brings to environmental conservation, social equity, and governance improvement. For instance, if a blockchain project is designed to reduce carbon emissions, the narrative should explain how the technology achieves this through more efficient process management or through the facilitation of renewable energy markets.

It is also crucial to focus on tangible outcomes that resonate with the audience. This means going beyond abstract promises to demonstrate clear, measurable impacts such as quantifiable reductions in emissions, documented improvements in labor conditions along supply chains, or enhanced compliance with data protection regulations. Real-world examples and case studies play a vital role in this context. They not only serve to ground the narrative in reality but also provide proof of concept, showcasing the successful application of blockchain technology in achieving desired ESG outcomes. For example, a blockchain initiative might involve a case study where the technology was used to trace the supply chain of agricultural products. The story could detail how the blockchain provided transparency from the farm to the consumer, ensuring that all products were sustainably sourced and workers were paid fair wages, thereby addressing social and governance aspects of ESG.

These narratives should be told in a manner that connects emotionally with the audience. They should paint a vivid picture of the challenges faced before the implementation of the blockchain solution and the subsequent improvements, making the impact feel real and substantial. This emotional connection can be incredibly persuasive, transforming stakeholders from passive observers to active supporters and advocates for the initiative.

In crafting these stories, it is important to use language that is clear and accessible, avoiding overly technical jargon that could alienate those unfamiliar with blockchain technology. The use of compelling visuals, infographics, and videos can also help illustrate complex processes in a straightforward and engaging way, further enhancing the narrative's impact. Ultimately, a compelling story not only informs but also inspires. It mobilizes support, drives engagement, and underscores the transformative potential of blockchain initiatives in advancing ESG goals. By effectively communicating these stories, organizations can build trust and enthusiasm among their stakeholders, paving the way for broader acceptance and success of their blockchain projects.

To effectively reach and resonate with a varied audience, organizations involved in blockchain initiatives must strategically utilize a diverse array of communication channels. Traditional methods like press releases and annual reports offer a formal way to communicate key developments and summarize the year's activities, providing stakeholders with a comprehensive overview of the organization's progress and insights into future directions. These tools are essential for reaching professional and institutional stakeholders who prefer detailed, substantive reporting.

Complementing these traditional tools, digital platforms such as blogs, social media, and podcasts allow for more dynamic and continuous engagement. Blogs can serve as a platform for sharing longer-form content that delves deeper into specific aspects of a blockchain project, explaining complex ideas in an accessible format. Social media platforms are ideal for more frequent, informal interactions. They provide a space for real-time updates, quick insights, and community engagement through comments and direct messages, allowing for a two-way dialogue between the organization and its audience. Podcasts offer a unique avenue for storytelling, where longer discussions about blockchain technology's implications and interviews with thought leaders can help in cultivating a knowledgeable community. This format is particularly effective in reaching audiences who prefer auditory learning or want more in-depth discussion while on the go.

In utilizing these diverse channels, organizations can tailor their communication strategies to meet the specific preferences and needs of different audience segments, maximizing the impact and reach of their messages. Stakeholder engagement is a cornerstone of successful communication strategies in blockchain initiatives. It involves more than just informing; it's about creating a dialogue that fosters a deep sense of involvement and partnership. Regular updates and interactions with stakeholders, including investors, customers, regulatory bodies, and the wider community, are crucial. These communications should be transparent and informative, providing stakeholders with a clear view of the project's progress, its challenges, and its successes.

Engagement can be significantly enhanced through interactive platforms such as webinars, workshops, and public forums. Webinars and workshops offer a structured setting for presenting detailed information and training stakeholders on new developments or features within the blockchain project. They also allow for real-time feedback and Q&A sessions, which can address stakeholders' concerns directly and foster a greater understanding of the project.

Public forums, whether online or in person, provide a more open platform where a broader community can engage with the project's leaders. These forums are invaluable for gauging public sentiment, understanding the concerns of the community, and gathering insightful feedback that can guide future strategies.

Through these engagement efforts, organizations can build and maintain trust, ensure the relevance of their initiatives, and foster robust partnerships that support sustained growth and acceptance of blockchain technologies. This continuous dialogue ensures that stakeholders feel valued and heard, which is essential for collaborative success in the dynamic and often complex landscape of blockchain initiatives.

Transparency in communication, especially regarding the challenges faced and the lessons learned from blockchain initiatives, plays a critical role in building trust and credibility with stakeholders. By openly sharing the difficulties encountered along the way, an organization demonstrates its commitment to honesty and integrity. This openness is not just about admitting faults or setbacks but also about showing the proactive steps taken to overcome these hurdles. Detailing the specific challenges—whether they involve technological obstacles, regulatory compliance issues, or integration difficulties—and the strategies implemented to address them provides valuable insights to stakeholders. It reveals the organization's ability to problem-solve and adapt under pressure, qualities that are crucial for success in the ever-evolving blockchain landscape. Moreover, discussing lessons learned from these challenges is equally important as it shows a commitment to continuous improvement and learning. It helps stakeholders understand that the project is in a state of ongoing development and refinement, which can inspire confidence and support.

Establishing thought leadership is another powerful way to enhance the credibility of communications around blockchain initiatives. Thought leadership involves providing insightful commentary, expert analyses, and forward-looking perspectives that contribute not just to the narrative of a single project but to the broader discussion of blockchain's role in achieving Environmental, Social, and Governance (ESG) goals.

This can be achieved by participating actively in industry conferences, where leaders can present their findings, share their experiences, and engage with other experts in the field. Publishing scholarly articles in reputable journals or magazines also helps to disseminate knowledge and establish the organization's members as experts in blockchain technology. Additionally, collaborations with academic institutions or industry consortia can lead to groundbreaking research and innovative solutions that further the development of the blockchain sector.

Through these channels, organizations can highlight their contributions to advancing blockchain technology and its applications for ESG objectives. Thought leadership not only raises the profile of the individual or organization but also contributes to the collective knowledge base, encouraging innovation and adoption of blockchain across various sectors. By focusing on both highlighting the challenges and lessons learned, and leveraging thought leadership, organizations can foster a more informed and engaged stakeholder base. This approach not only bolsters the organization's reputation but also strengthens the overall blockchain ecosystem by promoting transparency, continuous learning, and informed discussion.

In the context of communicating blockchain initiatives, particularly those aligned with Environmental, Social, and Governance (ESG) goals, visual and interactive content plays a pivotal role in making complex information more accessible and engaging. The inherent complexities of blockchain technology can often be a barrier to understanding for those not intimately familiar with the field. Visual aids like infographics, videos, and interactive dashboards are instrumental in bridging this gap, transforming intricate data and abstract concepts into clear, engaging, and easily understandable formats.

Infographics are particularly effective for summarizing large amounts of data and showing relationships and patterns that might be less apparent in text-based descriptions. They can visually represent the flow of blockchain transactions, the impact of blockchain on reducing carbon emissions, or how blockchain improves supply chain transparency. By presenting information graphically, infographics can highlight key points and statistics, making the content not only more attractive but also easier to remember.

Videos take this a step further by adding a narrative and auditory elements to the visual experience, which can enhance engagement and retention of information. Videos can be used to tell the story of a blockchain project from conception to implementation, showcasing real-world applications and the tangible benefits of blockchain initiatives. They can explain technical processes in a step-by-step manner, demonstrate the functionality of a blockchain platform, or feature testimonials from stakeholders who have benefited from the project. Videos are also highly shareable across digital platforms, increasing the visibility and impact of the blockchain initiative.

Interactive dashboards offer an advanced tool for stakeholders who want to delve deeper into the data and explore the specifics of a blockchain project at their own pace. These dashboards can provide real-time data visualization, allowing users to manipulate variables to see different scenarios or to drill down into the data for more detailed views. For instance, an interactive dashboard could allow stakeholders to view the environmental impact of a product at each stage of its supply chain or to explore different data security measures and their effectiveness. Interactive tools engage users in a hands-on manner, promoting a deeper understanding and a more personalized exploration of the content.

Utilizing these visual and interactive content formats can significantly enhance the communication strategy of a blockchain initiative. They not only simplify complex information, making it more digestible for non-experts, but also engage users in a way that text alone often cannot. By making blockchain initiatives more accessible and understandable, organizations can foster a broader understanding of their projects' benefits and contributions to ESG goals, ultimately driving greater interest, investment, and collaboration.

Effective communication in blockchain initiatives, particularly those aimed at advancing Environmental, Social, and Governance (ESG) goals, is not a one-time effort but a dynamic, ongoing process that thrives on continuous feedback and adaptation. This iterative approach is crucial for ensuring that the communication strategies remain aligned with the evolving needs of the project and the expectations of its stakeholders. Regular evaluation and adaptation of communication tactics allow organizations to maintain relevance and maximize the impact of their messaging, thus enhancing stakeholder engagement and support.

The first step in this process is actively seeking and collecting feedback from various stakeholders. This can be accomplished through surveys, feedback forms, direct interviews, social media interactions, and other engagement tools that gather insights from investors, customers, community members, and regulatory bodies. Feedback should cover all aspects of the communication strategy, including clarity, effectiveness, relevance, and the emotional impact of the messaging. By understanding how different stakeholders perceive and react to the communication efforts, organizations can identify strengths to build upon and areas that need improvement.

Once feedback is collected, the next step is to analyze the data and implement necessary changes to the communication strategies. Adaptation might involve adjusting the tone, content, or channels of communication to better suit the audience's preferences and needs. For example, if feedback indicates that technical jargon is a barrier to understanding, the organization might simplify its language or use more visual aids to explain complex concepts. If certain platforms are not reaching the intended audience effectively, resources may be reallocated to more effective channels.

Adaptation also involves updating the content to reflect new developments within the project or changes in the external environment, such as regulatory updates or shifts in market dynamics. Keeping the communication content current and relevant not only informs stakeholders but also demonstrates the organization's commitment to transparency and accountability.

This process of feedback and adaptation is not linear but cyclical, requiring ongoing attention and refinement. Organizations should establish regular intervals for review and updates of their communication strategies, ensuring that they adapt to continuous changes in the project and its external environment. This iterative process helps in fine-tuning the approach, ensuring that the communication strategy not only keeps pace with the project's development but also resonates effectively with the evolving landscape of stakeholder expectations.

By engaging in this continuous process of feedback and adaptation, organizations can ensure that their communication strategies effectively convey the impacts of their blockchain initiatives in meeting ESG goals. This not only fosters a supportive environment for innovation but also demonstrates the transformative potential of blockchain technology in addressing critical global challenges. Furthermore, effective communication plays a pivotal role in captivating and retaining stakeholder interest, guiding them through the project's evolution, and inspiring them with stories of meaningful impact and progressive change. This dynamic approach to communication underscores the importance of adaptability and responsiveness, essential qualities for any organization aiming to lead in the rapidly evolving blockchain ecosystem. The essence of effective storytelling lies in the ability to weave together the various strands of a project—its challenges, achievements, and the vision driving it forward. Such narratives allow stakeholders to forge an emotional connection with the project's mission and trajectory. By sharing stories that encapsulate the hurdles overcome and the milestones reached, stakeholders can gain a deeper appreciation of the project's significance and the team's perseverance.

It is crucial for sustainability-focused narratives not only to discuss the challenges faced but also to spotlight the solutions and positive outcomes. This approach not only instills hope but also showcases the project's proactive stance in finding and implementing solutions. Such stories inspire stakeholders and demonstrate the tangible impacts of the blockchain initiative, reinforcing the project's role in driving meaningful change.

Authenticity in storytelling involves openly sharing the project's past shortcomings alongside its ongoing efforts to improve. This level of transparency is vital for building trust with stakeholders. It shows a genuine commitment to not just achieving goals but also to continuous improvement and honesty. This can strengthen stakeholder relationships and enhance their commitment to the project. Integrating visual elements such as images, videos, and infographics can significantly enrich the storytelling experience. Visuals capture attention and help convey complex information in an intuitive and engaging manner. They can make the blockchain project's impacts and processes more accessible to those who may not be familiar with the technical aspects of blockchain technology.

To maximize impact, it's important to tailor narratives to meet the specific interests and preferences of different stakeholder groups. Understanding what each segment of the audience cares about allows the stories to be more relevant and compelling. This customization ensures that the narratives not only inform but also resonate deeply with diverse groups, from investors to end-users. We have explored the critical role of effective communication in conveying the impacts of blockchain initiatives, especially those aimed at achieving Environmental, Social, and Governance (ESG) goals. A key takeaway is the importance of crafting compelling narratives that resonate with diverse audiences. By articulating how blockchain projects align with and advance ESG objectives, and by demonstrating tangible outcomes through real-world examples and case studies, organizations can make their initiatives more accessible and engaging.

The use of diverse communication channels is essential to reach a broad audience. Traditional and digital media each play crucial roles, with social media facilitating frequent updates and interactions, and detailed reports providing depth and substantiation. Engaging stakeholders through regular dialogue and interactive platforms ensures that they remain informed and involved, enhancing transparency and trust.

Highlighting both challenges and successes in these communications not only enhances credibility but also underscores the organization's commitment to honesty and improvement. Additionally, establishing thought leadership through insightful analysis and forward-looking perspectives positions the organization as a knowledgeable and influential voice in the blockchain community. Visual and interactive content is invaluable for clarifying complex concepts and demonstrating the impacts of blockchain more effectively. This approach can break down barriers to understanding and increase the accessibility of information to a broader, non-expert audience. Finally, the process of continuous feedback and adaptation ensures that communication strategies evolve in response to changing conditions and stakeholder feedback, maintaining relevance and effectiveness over time.

By integrating these strategies, blockchain initiatives can effectively communicate their value and impact, engaging stakeholders in a manner that is both informative and inspiring. Well-crafted stories not only share the journey of the blockchain project but also rally support for its vision and goals, fostering a supportive environment for innovation and demonstrating the transformative potential of blockchain technology in addressing global challenges. Through this approach, blockchain projects can inspire widespread participation and drive collective efforts towards a shared, sustainable future.

Chapter 10: The Future of Purpose-Driven Blockchain Leadership

As blockchain technology continues to evolve and integrate more deeply with Environmental, Social, and Governance (ESG) principles, the role of leadership within this domain is also transforming. Purpose-driven leadership is increasingly recognized as a critical component in navigating the complex interplay between technological innovation and sustainable development. This section explores the potential future pathways for leadership at the nexus of blockchain and ESG, offering speculations on how this role might develop in the coming years. Future leaders in the blockchain sector are recognizing the potential for this technology to directly address pressing global challenges, moving beyond its initial financial applications to become a powerful tool for sustainable development.

One of the key strategies involves developing blockchain platforms specifically designed to tackle social and environmental issues. For example, new blockchain systems could be created to enhance energy efficiency within industrial processes by providing a transparent, immutable record of energy usage and carbon emissions. This transparency not only helps companies monitor their impact but also allows them to share verifiable data with regulators and the public, promoting greater accountability and facilitating compliance with environmental standards.

Another significant application of blockchain in achieving ESG goals is improving supply chain transparency. By leveraging blockchain technology, companies can trace the origin and journey of products from raw materials to finished goods. This level of traceability ensures that products are sustainably sourced and that all participants in the supply chain adhere to fair labor practices and environmental regulations. For consumers, this means greater confidence in the products they purchase, and for companies, it means enhanced brand trust and loyalty.

Blockchain can also revolutionize the secure and equitable distribution of resources, particularly in underdeveloped or crisis-affected regions. For instance, blockchain platforms can be used to manage the distribution of humanitarian aid, ensuring that resources reach their intended recipients without interference or misappropriation. Similarly, blockchain could facilitate access to financial services for the unbanked populations, promoting financial inclusion and empowering individuals with tools for economic stability.

For leaders to effectively integrate ESG goals with blockchain's capabilities, they must possess a deep understanding of both blockchain technology and ESG principles. This involves continuous education and staying updated with the latest developments in both fields. Leaders must also be adept at identifying the intersection of ESG needs and blockchain capabilities, envisioning innovative solutions that harness the unique benefits of blockchain for sustainable impact.

The responsibility of future blockchain leaders extends beyond technical expertise; they must also champion ethical practices and sustainable development. This requires a visionary approach that seeks not just to exploit blockchain for economic gain but to utilize it as a tool for real and positive change. By fostering collaborations across industries, governments, and non-governmental organizations, leaders can drive the adoption of blockchain solutions that genuinely benefit society and the environment.

Integrating ESG goals with blockchain technology offers a promising path forward in addressing some of the world's most critical challenges. As this field matures, the role of leaders will be pivotal in steering blockchain innovations towards outcomes that promote not only technological advancement but also social equity, environmental sustainability, and good governance.

Ethical stewardship in blockchain involves more than adhering to existing regulations; it requires proactive leadership in setting new standards that prioritize transparency, accountability, and inclusivity. Leaders must ensure that blockchain technologies are used in ways that do not merely seek profit, but also foster societal good. This includes developing and implementing governance frameworks that enhance the transparency of blockchain operations, allowing stakeholders to track where and how blockchain systems are deployed, and ensuring that these activities are conducted in an ethical manner.

An integral part of ethical stewardship involves identifying and mitigating the potential risks associated with blockchain technology. These risks include privacy concerns, where the immutable nature of blockchain could conflict with the need to protect personal data in accordance with privacy laws like GDPR. Leaders must navigate these challenges by crafting policies that balance the benefits of blockchain's transparency with the necessity of protecting individual privacy. Inequality is another significant risk, as the benefits of blockchain could become concentrated in the hands of those who already have technological access and expertise. Ethical governance in this context means ensuring that blockchain deployments do not exacerbate social inequalities but rather promote inclusivity and accessibility. This may involve initiatives to enhance digital literacy, making blockchain technologies more accessible to underprivileged communities.

Environmental impact is also a crucial consideration. Some blockchain applications, particularly those that rely on energy-intensive consensus mechanisms like Proof of Work, have significant carbon footprints. Ethical stewardship requires leaders to consider environmentally friendly alternatives, such as Proof of Stake or other less energy-intensive technologies, to ensure that blockchain's environmental impact is managed responsibly.

The ultimate aim of ethical stewardship and robust governance in blockchain is to ensure that these technologies contribute positively to societal goals. This involves aligning blockchain deployments with broader Environmental, Social, and Governance (ESG) objectives to create not only economic value but also social and environmental benefits. Leaders must engage with a wide range of stakeholders, including regulators, community groups, and environmental organizations, to align blockchain projects with the public interest and foster a collaborative approach to governance.

Ethical stewardship in blockchain is not a static goal but a continuous process of improvement and adaptation. As blockchain technology evolves and its applications expand, leaders must remain vigilant and responsive to new ethical challenges and opportunities. This requires a commitment to ongoing learning, stakeholder engagement, and innovation in governance practices to ensure that blockchain remains a force for good in the rapidly evolving digital landscape. As blockchain technologies become increasingly integrated into societal and environmental systems, the role of ethical stewardship and robust governance frameworks becomes more critical. Future leaders in blockchain will need to set new standards in ethical deployment, craft policies to mitigate risks, and ensure that blockchain technology contributes positively to societal goals, all while fostering an environment of continuous ethical improvement and innovation.

The integration of blockchain with Environmental, Social, and Governance (ESG) initiatives is inherently complex, calling for a leadership approach that emphasizes collaboration and partnership. Future leaders in this field are expected to step beyond traditional corporate silos to cultivate ecosystems that encompass a wide array of expertise and perspectives. These ecosystems will likely include technologists, policymakers, social activists, and business leaders, each bringing unique insights that are crucial for the holistic development of blockchain solutions.

This collaborative network is essential not just for harnessing the full technological potential of blockchain but also for ensuring that its applications are ethically sound and aligned with broader societal values. For example, technologists can provide the necessary technical expertise to develop robust blockchain platforms, while social activists can offer insights into the social impacts of these technologies, ensuring that the solutions developed do not inadvertently exacerbate social inequalities.

Policymakers play a critical role in this ecosystem by helping to navigate the regulatory landscapes that blockchain projects must operate within. Their involvement ensures that blockchain solutions comply with existing laws and regulations, which is crucial for gaining public trust and acceptance. Moreover, policymakers can also advocate for the creation of new regulations that support innovative uses of blockchain while protecting public interests.

Business leaders, on the other hand, bring a pragmatic perspective to the table, focusing on scalability, sustainability, and economic viability. Their expertise in market dynamics and business operations is crucial for translating technological innovations into viable products and services that can achieve widespread adoption.

The success of blockchain in achieving ESG goals, therefore, hinges on the ability of these diverse groups to work together seamlessly. Collaborative leadership involves fostering a spirit of cooperation and open dialogue among all these stakeholders. It requires creating platforms where ideas can be freely exchanged and different viewpoints can be reconciled to develop solutions that are not only innovative but also equitable and just. These partnerships can accelerate the adoption of blockchain technologies by pooling resources, sharing risks, and synchronizing efforts across different sectors and disciplines. By working collaboratively, the various stakeholders can leverage their collective strengths to tackle the significant challenges at the intersection of technology, society, and the environment.

The future of blockchain in ESG initiatives will be shaped by leaders who can effectively build and manage these collaborative ecosystems. By fostering strong partnerships and encouraging a culture of collaboration, these leaders can ensure that blockchain technologies are developed and implemented in ways that are socially responsible, environmentally sustainable, and aligned with global efforts to achieve a more equitable world.

Leadership within the blockchain sector is evolving rapidly, requiring a progressive mindset that transcends conventional frameworks and approaches. The future demands leaders who not only push the technological boundaries of what blockchain can achieve but also pioneer new business models and strategic approaches that embed Environmental, Social, and Governance (ESG) principles at their core. This forward-thinking leadership is crucial in exploring and exploiting blockchain's potential to foster more inclusive and equitable systems.

One of the most transformative aspects of blockchain is its ability to facilitate decentralized and democratized systems that challenge traditional power structures and access paradigms. For instance, blockchain's application in decentralized finance (DeFi) represents a radical shift in how financial services are conceived and delivered. DeFi platforms use blockchain to create financial systems that are open to anyone with an internet connection, bypassing traditional financial institutions and removing barriers that typically prevent people from accessing financial services.

Leaders in the blockchain space are increasingly looking at DeFi not just as a tool for financial innovation but as a means to address significant social challenges, such as financial inclusion. By leveraging DeFi, blockchain leaders can provide essential financial services — from banking to lending to insurance — to the unbanked and underbanked populations around the world. This has the potential to empower millions by offering them control over their financial destinies and contributing to economic equality.

Innovating beyond traditional boundaries also involves rethinking business models to ensure they are sustainable and responsible. Blockchain leaders are beginning to design systems that inherently account for environmental impacts, social equity, and governance transparency. For example, some are pioneering "green blockchain" technologies that minimize environmental footprints, addressing one of the critical criticisms of traditional blockchain technologies.

These leaders are not working in isolation; they are building ecosystems that bring together diverse stakeholders to co-create solutions that are beneficial for society at large. This involves engaging with NGOs, government entities, and communities to ensure that blockchain solutions are not only innovative but also socially relevant and grounded in real-world needs.

This kind of leadership requires a deep understanding of both technology and the complex web of global social challenges. It also demands a commitment to continuous learning and adaptation, as the contexts in which blockchain is applied are dynamic and often unpredictable. Leaders must be adept at navigating this fluid landscape, ready to adjust their strategies in response to new information and shifting societal expectations. Leadership in the blockchain realm is increasingly about harnessing technology to drive positive change, breaking away from traditional practices to establish new norms that prioritize sustainability, inclusivity, and transparency. As blockchain continues to mature, the leaders who rise to the forefront will likely be those who can align innovative technological applications with profound societal impact, thereby redefining the boundaries of what is possible in the digital age.

As blockchain technology continues to advance into mainstream applications, the role of leaders in educating the public and advocating for responsible use becomes increasingly important. These leaders are not just technologists; they are also educators, community liaisons, and advocates for ethical practices. Their responsibilities extend beyond the technical development of blockchain to include fostering a broader understanding of the technology's potential impacts and benefits.

Education is a critical component of leadership in the blockchain space. As the technology permeates various sectors—from finance to healthcare to government—there is a growing need for the public to understand both the potential benefits and the risks associated with blockchain. Leaders must take an active role in demystifying the technology for a non-technical audience, explaining how it works, and highlighting its potential to drive positive change. This might involve organizing workshops, seminars, and webinars that cater to different segments of the public, providing resources that are accessible and engaging, and using case studies to illustrate real-world applications of blockchain.

Engagement with diverse communities ensures that the development of blockchain solutions is inclusive and considers a wide range of needs and perspectives. Leaders must reach out to underrepresented groups, listen to their concerns and aspirations, and incorporate their input into the blockchain development process. This inclusive approach not only enhances the relevance and acceptance of blockchain solutions but also helps prevent the technology from exacerbating existing inequalities. Engaging diverse communities involves building partnerships with community organizations, participating in forums and discussions in different cultural contexts, and ensuring that these communities have a voice in shaping the technology that may significantly impact their lives.

Advocacy for responsible and ethical regulation is another crucial area where blockchain leaders must focus their efforts. As blockchain technology evolves, there is a parallel need for regulatory frameworks that ensure its safe and ethical application. Leaders should engage with policymakers to help shape these regulations, advocating for laws that promote transparency, protect privacy, and ensure accountability within blockchain systems. At the same time, it is important to lobby against overly restrictive regulations that could stifle innovation. This delicate balance requires a deep understanding of both the technological and regulatory landscapes, as well as a clear vision of how blockchain can serve the greater good without causing unintended harm.

Leaders in the blockchain space must champion the responsible use of technology. This includes setting high standards for ethical practices within their own organizations and projects, such as ensuring data privacy, securing informed consent when data is collected, and implementing sustainability measures to mitigate environmental impacts. By setting an example in ethical technology use, leaders can influence the entire blockchain industry, driving it towards more responsible and sustainable practices.

By embracing these roles—educators, community engagers, regulators, and ethical advocates—leaders can ensure that blockchain technology is developed and used in ways that are beneficial for society as a whole. They can help build a foundation of trust and understanding around blockchain, which is essential for its long-term success and acceptance.

The regulatory landscape for blockchain is expected to evolve significantly in the coming years. Purpose-driven leaders will need to be agile and proactive in adapting to these changes, ensuring that their projects remain compliant while continuing to advance ESG objectives. This will require a deep understanding of both local and global regulatory environments and the ability to navigate them effectively. The future of leadership in the blockchain sector will undoubtedly require a delicate balance between advanced technical knowledge and a strong ethical compass. As blockchain technology promises to reshape many aspects of our societies and economies, leaders who can integrate ESG principles into their projects will be pivotal in ensuring that this technology fulfills its potential as a force for good. The journey ahead for blockchain leaders is both challenging and filled with unprecedented opportunities to drive meaningful change.

As blockchain technology continues to mature and intersect more significantly with global challenges, the need for a forward-thinking approach in integrating blockchain with purpose-driven leadership becomes increasingly important. This integration is crucial for achieving impactful results that extend beyond financial gains to include meaningful societal and environmental benefits. Here's how leaders can cultivate a forward-thinking mindset and harness the potential of blockchain to drive substantial positive change.

Leaders should begin by visioning the broader potential of blockchain technology. This involves imagining future scenarios where blockchain can address significant societal and environmental challenges, from climate change to social inequality. By envisioning these possibilities, leaders can identify strategic opportunities where blockchain can be applied to make a tangible difference. This forward-thinking approach requires not only creativity and innovation but also a deep understanding of both the technology and the specific issues it might solve.

Blockchain's potential is best realized when combined with insights and expertise from various fields. Leaders should foster collaborations that bridge technology with other disciplines such as environmental science, social research, and public policy. These cross-disciplinary collaborations can inspire innovative solutions that are both technologically feasible and aligned with real-world needs. By working together, experts from different fields can create blockchain solutions that are more comprehensive and far-reaching.

Engaging a diverse group of stakeholders is essential for forward-thinking leadership. This includes not just investors and developers but also end-users, community leaders, and regulators. Effective stakeholder engagement involves active listening, continuous feedback, and genuine collaboration. This approach ensures that different perspectives are considered in the development of blockchain projects, enhancing their relevance and effectiveness.

Leaders should also advocate for regulatory frameworks that adapt to the rapid advancements in blockchain technology while safeguarding public interest. By engaging with policymakers and participating in legislative processes, leaders can help shape regulations that encourage innovation while protecting users and the environment. A forward-thinking leader anticipates regulatory changes and prepares their projects to adapt swiftly.

To stay ahead, leaders should be open to integrating blockchain with other cutting-edge technologies such as AI, IoT, and big data analytics. This integration can enhance the capabilities of blockchain applications, making them more intelligent, efficient, and scalable. Leaders need to be knowledgeable about these technologies and proactive in exploring how they can be synergistically combined with blockchain to enhance project outcomes. A forward-thinking approach involves a commitment to continuous learning and improvement. Blockchain technology and its applications are constantly evolving. Leaders must stay informed about the latest developments and trends in the field to guide their teams and projects effectively. Investing in ongoing education and professional development for themselves and their teams can help maintain a competitive edge and foster a culture of innovation.

By adopting these strategies, leaders can ensure that their use of blockchain technology is not only innovative and technically proficient but also ethically grounded and socially impactful. The future of blockchain leadership lies in the ability to anticipate change, inspire collaboration, and commit to making a positive difference in the world.

As we stand at the intersection of technological innovation and global sustainability challenges, blockchain technology emerges as a pivotal force in shaping the future of Environmental, Social, and Governance (ESG) leadership. The unique attributes of blockchain—its transparency, security, and immutability—make it an invaluable tool in the pursuit of a more sustainable and equitable world.

Blockchain's potential to revolutionize industries by enhancing transparency and accountability is profound. In the environmental sector, it can track carbon emissions and verify sustainable practices across global supply chains. Socially, blockchain facilitates inclusivity by providing unbanked populations access to financial services and ensuring that aid reaches intended recipients without corruption. In terms of governance, blockchain can help enforce ethical standards and compliance across organizations and industries, fostering a higher level of integrity and public trust.

The power of blockchain extends beyond its technological capabilities; it lies in how leaders choose to deploy this technology. To truly harness its potential, leaders must prioritize purpose and ethical governance in their blockchain initiatives. This means designing projects that not only drive economic value but also contribute positively to society and the environment. Leaders must approach blockchain with a commitment to ethical standards, ensuring that technological advancements are matched with strong moral frameworks. This commitment should be evident in every aspect of blockchain implementation—from the planning and development stages to execution and community engagement.

As we stand on the brink of technological revolution brought forth by blockchain, the call to action for current and future leaders is unmistakably clear. This technology is not merely a mechanism for financial growth or operational efficiency; it represents a profound opportunity to catalyze real, sustainable change across multiple facets of society. Leaders are thus urged to embrace and harness this potential responsibly.

Leaders must innovate with a conscience, developing blockchain solutions that provide tangible benefits not just economically but also socially and environmentally. It is imperative that these innovations consider the broader impact on the planet and its inhabitants, ensuring solutions contribute positively and mitigate any potential adverse effects.

Using blockchain to enhance transparency should be a priority. By making data more accessible and verifiable, leaders can build a foundation of trust among stakeholders. This transparency not only clarifies operations but also strengthens accountability, making it easier for everyone involved—from consumers to regulators—to trust in the processes and products enhanced by blockchain technologies.

It is essential that the benefits of blockchain technology are felt by all layers of society, especially those who are traditionally marginalized or excluded from the digital economy. Leaders must ensure that blockchain implementations do not deepen existing divides but rather serve to bridge them, providing equal opportunities for access and benefits.

Leaders in the blockchain space must set an example by both advocating for and adhering to the highest ethical standards. This includes respecting user privacy, ensuring secure systems, and promoting fair practices. By championing these values, leaders can guide the industry towards a more ethical and equitable direction.

Maintaining an ongoing dialogue with all stakeholders is crucial. This includes not just partners and regulators but also the wider community that will be affected by blockchain technologies. Engagement ensures that blockchain initiatives are well-rounded, considerate of various perspectives, and aligned with broader societal goals. Leaders who respond to this call to action will not only shape the future of blockchain technology but will also guide the world towards greater sustainability and equity. Embracing this role with commitment, innovation, and a deep sense of responsibility will ensure that the legacy of blockchain technology is marked by significant and positive global impacts, steered by purposeful leadership and ethical governance. This proactive approach will pave the way for pioneering a sustainable and ethical future with blockchain, setting a standard for how technology can and should benefit humanity.

www.ingramcontent.com/pod-product-compliance
Lightning Source LLC
Chambersburg PA
CBHW052259220526
45471CB00001B/409